CHESAPEAKE BAY ADVENTURES

TALES FROM THE EASTERN SHORE

C.L. MARSHALL

THE
History
PRESS

Published by The History Press
Charleston, SC
www.historypress.com

Copyright © 2023 by C.L. Marshall
All rights reserved

All images by Locked In Productions unless otherwise noted.

First published 2023

Manufactured in the United States

ISBN 9781467153539

Library of Congress Control Number: 2022947992

Notice: The information in this book is true and complete to the best of our knowledge. It is offered without guarantee on the part of the author or The History Press. The author and The History Press disclaim all liability in connection with the use of this book.

All rights reserved. No part of this book may be reproduced or transmitted in any form whatsoever without prior written permission from the publisher except in the case of brief quotations embodied in critical articles and reviews.

THE CHESAPEAKE PROVIDES. It provides the obvious, such as crabs, fish and water-related activities. Of greater intrinsic value is the bonds it creates. On it and through it, the lives of many are forever linked. Shared experience is the common thread that changes the lives of those who choose to venture forth for adventure. Whether a quiet dinner cruise with the family, gunning for bluebills on the leeward side of a windswept point or dunking minnows adorned with bobbers for crappie in its upper reaches, the Chesapeake is central to many.

Each of us can play a part in taking care of her. Each of us is responsible for passing it along to those who come behind us in better condition than we found it. As the demands we place on her increase, our resolve should increase proportionally. Let's do our job to take care of her.

As I stood there at a rented podium staring at the camouflage-clad group assembled to say farewell to my father, I could only smile. Several hundred folks had assembled down on Creek Point in Saxis, Virginia, to watch the sun set on a life well lived. In a short eighty years, he'd been many things to many people. To me, he was just Dad. To him I owe my love for all things outdoors.

CONTENTS

Contents

PREFACE

E ach of the books in the Chesapeake series is meant to provide a common thread among those who take full advantage of what it has to offer. Though this collection of short stories is based on personal experience, it's my hope that familiarity will be found in these pages that rekindle memories of the reader's experiences. There's been a predictable transition through the series. This book takes a strong introspective into the things that cross a shoreman's mind as age creeps into the equation. Things become more difficult. Relationships are held in higher regard. Time spent on the Bay is treasured a bit more, and these few stories will hopefully revive long-lost memories. They are about the off-the-grid places we hold sacred, the fire that drives us into the storm, the strings that tether to those who came before us and the time spent reliving the bounty the Bay provides.

Image by Joyce Northam.

THAT DAMN CELL PHONE

Staring out over the decoys, he began to take stock of just how much waterfowl hunting had changed during the half century since his first trip. A few of the remaining wooden decoys he used to hunt over now ride on the mantel above his fireplace. Others are scattered throughout his home and garage. Electric-start engines, waterproof shot shells and huge advances in clothing have enabled him to continue to engage in his passion as the years passed. He still carried his old humpback A-5.

Sitting just to his right, silently scanning his social media on his cell phone, was his son, home from college over Christmas break. Duck hunting—or any hunting, for that matter—remained a common bond that he and his father shared. The elder enjoyed the time spent alone with his son and used it to discuss matters that could not be discussed at home.

The introduction of the cellular device into the duck blind was difficult for the elder hunter to fathom. It seemed absurd to allow entrance of a device into their private time that would bring outsiders inside their inner sanctum. The intrusion, from his perspective, was sacrilegious in a hunting scenario. The junior of the two fully understood the "look" he received from his elder and stuffed the phone in his chest pocket. In this instance, the "look" wasn't enough.

"Put that damn thing away. Next thing you know they'll be tracking us with it. I'll never understand why you stare into it so much. There's a lot more to look at out here," he said, pointing to the horizon. For him, hunting was a method of escape from the daily grind. Cellular intrusion would not be tolerated.

Sitting in the deer stand alone, the son found the perfect place for personal reflection. The thoughts of his job, kids, wife, bills and plans intermittently crept into his head, but the pressing item that fueled these interruptions and that weighed on him most was his father. Age isn't always kind, and in this case, it was downright evil. Memory and pulmonary issues had taken away his father's ability to join in the hunt. His lucid moments were filled with talk of experiences afield and instruction offered about all things true Eastern Shoremen treasure.

Now, the first weekend in January, waterfowl season was halfway through. Deer season was closing in just a few hours. The younger hunter had gone out a handful of times, but it was the first year in his outdoor life that he had not been joined at some point by the hunting companion of his formative years. He missed hunting with his father. They still talked about it daily. They discussed the best options for the given wind, where the bigger bucks on the farm should be and the latest successes and failures.

It was odd that though time and age had taken away many things from his father, such as where he went for lunch or how to get back home from the Walmart, when the topic turned to hunting, he remained sharp as a tack. Though his dad was not with him in the stand or blind, he was always part of the hunt. At precisely 6:30 p.m. each night, they'd talk about the events of the day. He looked forward to that daily chat.

As the sun dropped below the tree line on the last day of the Virginia rifle season, two does scampered out of the woods to his right. Immediately, he raised his binoculars and began scanning the wood line where they exited. Chances were good that there'd be another popping out soon. His attention focused on the pair of does to the right, he did not see the deer they'd dubbed "Whiskey" step into the field to his left. With long G1 antlers and G2s that angled slightly inward, his rack looked something like a W. This, along with his darker color that matched a glass of straight whiskey, earned him his moniker.

Easing back in this chair, the sight of Whiskey casually strolling through the field almost took his breath. He and his father had pursued this animal almost exclusively for the last three years. Through all this time, they'd only had two other encounters with him. Once he stood broadside at three hundred yards staring back toward the box, seemingly knowing that he was safely out of range of the muzzleloader. The second occurred during the previous year's rifle season on what proved to be the elder's last hunt. Coming in on a string, he refused to provide a shot, his body shielded by a pair of formidable pine trees with only his eyes, snout and antlers protruding

There are many apps that help the hunting effort, but nothing replaces hard work.

from the western side of the tree. The length of time this showdown lasted grows with each telling of the tale.

This day seemed different. Whiskey, now nearing six years of age, was showing signs of his age. His back sagged a bit, his muzzle and left side were scarred from battle and this year's rut had taken more weight off him than he'd been able to put back on before the New Year. At a distance of just 125 yards, he again stood broadside, nibbling gently on the new winter wheat, occasionally raising his impressive antlers for an inquisitive look around.

Instinct and training took over. The gun was slowly raised, breathing controlled, safety clicked off and the shot taken. As the trigger was squeezed, he knew the shot was good. The old warrior absorbed the shock of the bullet, kicked his hind legs high in the air, quickly covered the fifty yards of wheat and disappeared into the woods on the same trail on which he entered the field.

Sitting in the stand, the reality of what had just occurred began to become clear in the hunter's mind. His first emotion was emptiness. He wished that his father could have been there to share in this experience. Emotion overcame him as he sat in the stand reliving the experience. Gathering himself, he climbed down from the stand. Reaching into his chest pocket, he extracted his flashlight and cell phone. He couldn't wait to tell his father what had occurred and quickly dialed his number.

Upon answering, his father quipped the usual post-hunt question: "Well?"

Sitting on the base of the stand, the details of the shot were meticulously discussed. With the sun now long gone, a decision had to be made whether to let Whiskey rest for the night or to go in after him right now.

"Son, if you've hit him like you say you've hit him, then go get him. Only you know."

With the phone now on speaker, he went to the spot where the bullet had impacted Whiskey. "Do you see blood at the point of impact? What color is it? Are there bubbles in it? Are there any bone fragments in it? Is there a blood trail? Is it a consistent trail, or is it the result of spurts? Did the deer go down?" and many other details were discussed. Though the two were not together, the event was shared through the magic of 4G.

The blood trail was followed to the woods. No detail was too small to discuss. It was obvious that the elder was fully engaged in the event and that it had significant meaning to him.

"Is there blood spatter on the ground, or is it sprayed on the trees? How far up on the tree trunks? Is it a steady flow? Good, he should be just ahead.

The feeling of getting hands on the antlers of a buck hunted for many years is very gratifying and somewhat emotional.

He couldn't have gone far. We'll find him," his father enthusiastically offered. He was involved the chase.

The beam of light caught a spot of white lying just fifty yards inside the woods. A few more quick steps and the culmination of three years' effort lay in a small clearing, propped up against a log.

"There he is! There he is! We did it," the junior exclaimed in the cell phone, acknowledging his father's efforts in this event as much as his.

"Hot damn, boy! You need some help? Bring that thing by here so I can put my hands on him," the old man exclaimed.

Thanks to dry weather, the deer was quickly loaded into the back of the Silverado. Seventeen minutes later, the other part of the hunting team ambled out of the warm confines of his house and didn't go directly to the deer to which he'd devoted so much time hunting. Instead, he grabbed his son and hugged him tightly.

"Thanks for including me in this hunt. I guess those damn cell phones are good for something after all."

ENDINGS AND NEW BEGINNINGS

As the 20221–22 duck season wore on, the grind began to lose some of its allure. In normal years, the frigid temps of January signaled the transition of our efforts from puddle ducks to divers. Cold weather, ice and diver shooting historically consumed our January trips.

This year was much different. The places that previously held ducks held ducks no more. Land had sold to new owners from across the waters, and two of my more productive blinds had been lost. The public areas that black ducks frequented were empty. Trip after trip had Finley and me staring into empty skies. By all accounts, this year was a bust.

As the end of the season drew near, the weather gods threw us a little bone by providing us with a bit of colder weather. The birds didn't show up in any appreciable numbers, but there was enough to get the dog wet a time or two on each trip. Knowing that the end was near, my trips became more frequent.

Though current regulations allowed only goose per person, we'd found a spot on open water that consistently provided just that. An afternoon shoot lasting about an hour would yield a goose or two and the opportunity for a little late-season work with the dog. It wasn't exactly fast and furious, but it was something.

Maryland's season provided a bonus day on the last day of January. My youngest son and I made plans to see the season close sitting in the sixteen-foot riveted johnboat staring over a couple dozen floating goose stools.

After dropping into the river just about four o'clock, the twenty-year-old Yamaha skiff sputtered to life after a dozen or so tugs on the rope.

Pressure can be applied to blind mates when a single appears over the decoys. A good shot will be rewarded with appropriate commentary. A miss will live forever.

"Feathering" the manual choke to keep her running, we slowly backed out of the ramp only to have her choke out when shifted to forward. A couple more pulls and she again was running. Now up on plane, we made our way against the strong ebbing tide. Unobstructed by any waterfowl, the sun shone brightly in a Carolina blue sky as we made our way upriver.

The falling tide had exposed a mudflat extending some twenty feet into the river at the point where we intended to hunt. That stake was certainly out of play. Heading back downriver to our other stake, we found enough water to float the rig just uptide of a sharp bend where we'd historically had success in previous years. In short order, we had a dozen and a half floating goose decoys out along with four black ducks for good measure. The blind was set up, guns loaded and we were hunting.

As the first five minutes passed, we watched a full third of our decoys drag out to the deeper part of the river and begin drifting downriver at about three knots. Typical luck for the year. We waited another five minutes to see if any more would be carried away by the strong ebbing tide and then made the decision to make adjustments. Picking up nearly half our rig, we re-deployed in the shallower water not as far off the bank as we would have liked, but they were back in the game. With only forty or so minutes left in this lackluster season, it felt as though we were just going through the motions.

Pulling the trigger on this closing day would just be a bonus. As my youngest seed grows older, demands on his time, work and other distractions dictate that our joint hunting trips annually become less frequent. On this afternoon, in spite of all that seemingly was against us, we were content to just spend a couple hours together.

We watched as another couple decoys floated around the corner. We'd pick them up in about fifteen minutes. A few wood ducks cruised along the river shore. The occasional mallard would rise over the marsh and settle back in the hinterlands just as quickly. The balmy conditions weren't perfect for gunning, but it was the last day. We were going to stick it out to the end.

With fifteen minutes or so to go in the season, a few geese began to make their way from the fields to the river for their nightly siesta. The first visible flock cruised behind us, showing no interest. Several others followed the same flight plan. As the sun dipped behind the trees, we decided that we'd had enough of this season. The guns were unloaded, blind bags zipped, painter untied from the blind stake and we declared this season dead and gone.

Another dozen geese passed behind us, a little closer than the rest. The Eastern Shoreman was still around my neck, and I hit it a couple times

Thick, nontypical, full of character and tagged. This ol' boy fell due to the temptation of a mature doe nibbling on bean stubble.

just for the hell of it. In unison, the dozen turned as one toward the decoys, set their wings and began a rather steep descent. Scrambling behind the pop-up blind, we worked quickly to unsheathe our weapons.

"Are they still coming?" Parker whispered. Peering through the parted brushes of the blind, I could see the dozen now on the deck, wings outstretched, gliding effortlessly toward the decoys at a distance of sixty yards.

"Yep," was all he needed to hear.

We each managed to get one of our "cripple" shells in our guns as the dozen began to backpedal just outside the decoys, feet dangling just above the tannic acid–stained water.

"Let's kill two!" was the call.

Our shots rang out in unison as the remainder of the sun fell beyond the horizon. Two geese lay still on the surface, quickly drifting, not unlike our decoys. Our season was now complete and seemingly not the total loss that we'd thought it was just over an hour ago. Our memories weren't made with the quantity of shots but in the quality of the day's events.

It was an excellent way to end the season, taking some of the sting out of the days when we had no such experience. Picking up the decoys, we immediately began talking about the coming season, with the past closed just ten minutes ago. The conversation brimmed with optimism, new plans and hope. In all things, hunting included, in each end there's a new beginning.

We're going to bust 'em next year.

SOME DAYS

It was a hunt that was hastily thrown together. My workday had ended, leaving me with just over two hours before the sun was scheduled to fall from the sky. The wife was working late. All things pointed to a quiet afternoon puddle duck hunt.

The skiff was quickly attached to the truck. A brief once-over of the decoys assured me that there were a dozen black ducks and an equal amount of teal boxed haphazardly lying in the front of the boat. All appeared good to go. Warm socks, jeans and the same cold gear and base layer that I'd worn for the past week slid on like an old friend. Just that quickly, I was out of the house, heading south to Drum Bay for a scheduled meeting with Mr. Black Duck.

A brief stop at Goose Creek provided the necessary fuel, coffee and sundries for the scheduled two-hour trip. Fifteen minutes later, I was donning waders and my overcoat at the boat ramp. Things had gone according to plan to this point. Things were about to change.

Normally, the skiff slides right off the trailer. This time, the blind material got hung in the side stations of the trailer, ripping one side nearly clean off. Five minutes and a dozen or so electrical ties and we were back in the game. The old pull start found it hard to catch spark, but after nearly twenty-five pulls of the cord, she finally sputtered to life. As she roughly idled, I pushed the bow around to face the creek before hopping off the sandbar and engaging forward gear. The old Yammy immediately cut off. Another half dozen yanks were required to revive the old girl. We were on our way.

It was a queer wind for December. Southeast at ten isn't something that we normally have to contend with. This would force me to tie a rig on unfamiliar turf. No big deal; I was just glad to be out. After I worked the throttle to full, the light aluminum boat broke out on plane quickly. A quartering sea made the first ten minutes of the trip uncomfortable. Soon, however, she found the shelter of the distant shore and ran quickly in the calmer water. Rounding War Point, I eased off plane and began to search for a suitable place to make my afternoon play. Immediately, the motor shut off. I'd picked something up on the propeller, but I couldn't get the motor to tilt up. No matter how hard I pulled on that thing, there was absolutely no give. Finally, with my boot braced against the transom and pulling with all my might, the engine cowling gave way, sending me sprawling backward, tripping across the bench seat and landing rather gracefully among the decoys. Thank the Lord they were there. They certainly made my landing a bit easier. I'm sure it wasn't a pretty sight.

Upon righting myself and making sure that I was still OK, cursing, I reattached the engine cowling. Seeing that it was going to stay put, my attention moved to the problem at hand. A quick observation divulged the problem. The new bow line I'd installed recently was a bit too long and had wrapped around the wheel. Instinctively, I reached for my push pole. It wasn't anywhere to be found; I'd left it in the other boat. Glancing up, I could see the windward bank quickly approaching. Leaning over the motor and shoulder deep in the frigid water, I began the task of unwrapping the half-inch line from the wheel. My added weight beyond the stern was just enough to enable the first couple waves to break over the stern. Now soaked on my entire left side, I slowly began to make my way in unwrapping the thick line from around the wheel.

Finally finishing just as the skiff washed up on the bank, I quickly jumped on the firm marsh and gave her a push. Finding enough water to fire the engine, she came to life on the eighth pull. Again, feathering the choke, she coughed along away from the bank toward a leeward point that looked promising. On this beautiful afternoon's rising tide, I haphazardly tossed out the dozen black duck decoys and half of the teal upwind of the big ducks. The small gut just inside the point looked like a fine place to hide. The bow was nosed as far as the twenty-five-horsepower Yamaha could push it into the muddy creek. Upon once again choking out, the engine's lower unit was pegged into the mud.

With the blind popped up and several pieces of fast grass properly placed, I was pretty pleased with how the spread looked. With just over an hour to hunt before sunset, I poured a cup of coffee and took in the surroundings. A pair of black ducks quietly rose and fell a few hundred yards away. The occasional bufflehead rounded the point well within range. On the other side of the cove, a band-tailed hawk slowly rode the currents a dozen yards off the grass looking for dinner. It was a grand place to spend the afternoon.

My mental vacation was interrupted by the sound made by the collision of air and wings. Placing my coffee cup on the seat just to my right, I slowly reached for my weapon. The pair of baldpates danced against the northwest wind just outside the decoys. The sound made by my coffee cup hitting the metal floor of the boat thwarted the birds' thoughts of decoying nicely. I didn't even rise, just watched as they flared away in the wind.

Fumbling to retrieve my cup, I finally got a finger in it and placed it in the corner of my blind bag. A drake bufflehead was the first thing I saw as I again joined the hunt. An incoming dark spot to the left then got my full attention. Remaining otherwise motionless, my right hand again reached for my Franchi. Effortlessly gliding under the southeast wind, the black duck continued his inbound flight. His orange feet outstretched, wings backpedaling, he quickly made himself comfortable alongside his new fake friends. Happily paddling along, quacking occasionally, the new arrival was quite comical to watch. His evening sabbatical was interrupted as the combination of rising tide and southeast wind worked together to free my boat from its position lodged in the small creek. As we quietly drifted out of our secluded perch, our visitor became increasingly alarmed. A couple loud quacks and he was gone.

With no push pole to remedy the situation, six pulls of the rope were required to fire the engine. I pushed the skiff as far as possible up the small gut, again pegging the lower unit into the mud to hold us in place.

Taking my place on the center seat, I poured another cup of coffee and resumed my mental vacation. The day hadn't gone as planned, but that was OK. I wasn't going to let the day's problems ruin this afternoon. Again, lost in my own thoughts of the day, seven dark objects appeared from behind me. In unison they turned back toward my meager spread. Securing my cup and gripping my gun, I made ready for the opportunity. As I was shooting from a seated position, my eye found the greenhead in the center. Reflex sent him tumbling to the water. The two blacks below the greenhead began their escape, held in place by the light southeast breeze. A single shot placed both beside the floating greenhead. The old gun was relieved of its third shell and placed in its case. A final cup was poured, calls and pocket shells were placed

Effort provides results. Today's hunters find good technology helps.

in the blind bag and the Stanley thermos secured. My hunting day was over, but my experience was not.

Finishing the cup and folding down the blind, I made ready to leave. The Yamaha had other plans. A dozen pulls of the string provided no ignition. When it finally sputtered to life, I made my way to the decoys, the retrieval of which was made extremely difficult without a pole or reverse gear. What should have taken five minutes took a frustrating twenty. Under a full moon, the ride back to the ramp was uneventful.

The two hours spent in Drum Bay on this afternoon were fraught with misadventure. Many things didn't go as planned—some from poor planning, some due to lack of preparation. Some of the misfortune was due to mechanical failure. But in that one instant when years of training, instinct and opportunity intersected, all was good in the universe. Not everything always goes as plan.

When duck hunting, that's about the only thing you can count on.

THE FIRE

Most of the workday Friday was spent constantly checking Weather Underground on my phone. Friday morning's hunt was over not long after it started, as our three-man limit of wood ducks was banged out in less than an hour. The forecast was for winds increasing in the afternoon to nearly gale force, snow and all the things waterfowlers look forward to.

The snow was scheduled to start around nine o'clock, and my trip down coastal Delmarva showed many more fowl had found their way to the area. Temperatures were slated to be in the single digits in the morning, with wind chills around zero. It was still holding at a balmy forty degrees as of 3:30 p.m., and the skiff was prepared for an afternoon goose hunt before the front moved through.

Having limited on ducks in the morning, Canada geese seemed to be the logical afternoon choice. I felt as though I knew where we'd find success, and two of us set out to find that limit as well. Around 4:15 p.m., the last of the decoys had splashed in the dark river water, the boat was hidden properly and the guns were loaded. We'd been there about fifteen minutes—the first cup of coffee hadn't even had a chance to get cold—when the first single signaled his arrival. Some three hundred yards out, he'd seen the decoys, found them acceptable and made a decision to join the party just twenty yards off the river shore.

As he dropped below the reedy shoreline, we lost sight of him momentarily. He was quickly located one hundred yards out, wings outstretched and effortlessly gliding toward the decoys. My hunting partner properly dispatched our visitor, and Finley made a retrieve of goose arguably about the same size as the little chocolate Lab.

With the first goose delivered to hand, our second customer appeared from behind us, hooking around directly in front of the decoys and beginning a quick vertical descent. I decided to take the shot at about thirty yards. Finley saw the entire show and once again made an excellent retrieve. It was a goose hunter's dream: in quickly, a quick limit and out before the goose start coming to the river in earnest, providing the opportunity for the next day's hunt. And the next day had the makings of being something special.

The alarm didn't get a chance to go off, as I was watching the time count down to 4:15 a.m. With coffee brewing, I handled the morning chores and emerged in the kitchen dressed as the last of the love dripped into the Yeti cup.

A thick blanket of snow covered the ground and the truck. The gunning skiff had remained hooked to the truck but kept shelter in the garage free from snow and ice. Waddling out through the snow, I quickly noticed the sting in the air. Wind chill temp had to be near the predicted zero. It was uncomfortable knocking the loose snow off the truck. Starting the engine, I noticed the temperature gauge reading eleven. That's a harsh number. With the defrost engaged, I made my way through the snow to the garage. Proper hunting apparel was donned, gear was gathered and stowed in the boat and preparations were made to begin the trek to the dock.

But there was a different feeling to this morning's hunt. Normally, these were the days that I lived for. Wind, ice, snow and bitter cold were all obstacles for many but represented opportunity for me. Forty-five years of waterfowl hunting experience made me anxious for the opportunity that lay before me. Forty-five years of waterfowl hunting had also taken its toll on my body. Though I often hunt alone, there was a bit of anxiety about taking today's trip. A limit should be almost certain. It would be a welcome change from the duckless skies thus far in the season.

Now properly clothed to face the elements, Finley and I made our way through the snow to the truck. Somewhat warmed by the defroster, we slowly crunched our way out of the drive. Making new trails through the snow, we slowly made our way toward the ramp. In the early morning hour, it was difficult to tell the road from adjacent fields as the windswept drifts made it all look the same. Yet slowly we crept along the road. A trip that normally took fifteen minutes took thirty on this morning. When I arrived at the ramp, it was no surprise that I was the only one with plans on venturing out in this harsh weather.

Wind, ice, snow and rough seas are part of the appeal of waterfowl hunting.

For some strange reason, I didn't make the turn to back the small aluminum skiff down the ramp, instead pulling headlong perpendicular to the river. Blowing snow made it difficult to see one hundred yards from my position. Legal shooting time was still forty minutes away. Opening the driver's side door, which was on the leeward side of the northwest wind, I summoned the dog out for a bathroom break. Finley leaped from the driver's seat with all the vigor expected in a three-year-old Lab. After nosing around in the snow for a bit, he finally found a place suitable for him to do his business. Upon completion, he returned to my side. I signaled him to load back into the truck. He gave a puzzled look and then hopped back in.

The two of us sat there, just staring out into the cold. The thought of spending the next couple hours out in these conditions all of a sudden didn't seem so appealing. I figured I'd wait a few minutes until visibility improved. Once again slipping out of the truck, I began to make my way back to the boat where my old Stanley was stowed in my blind bag. The full force of the twenty-mile-per-hour wind, snow and bitter cold caught me a bit off guard as I stepped from behind the shelter of the truck. Snatching the whole blind bag from the boat, I quickly scurried back to the confines of the truck. The warmth of the coffee was welcomed.

I'd thought that if another hunter showed up we might join forces. Faint hues of pink began to show from the east. Fin and I sat silently staring at the wind-whipped snow absent of headlights in the growing morning light. The desire to go just wasn't there. As much as I tried to push myself to make this trip, there was something that just told me it wasn't a good idea. I went with my gut and poured a second cup of coffee, watching a snowy sunrise over the Pocomoke River. There'd be other trips, I told myself. There'd be more chances to make memories afield with my dog. Hopefully there'd be more time, more chances, more birds in our future. They'd have to wait for more amenable climes. There'd be no hunting for us on this day.

I suppose the fire has begun to fade.

THE BLACK DUCK SHOT

The temperature had dropped nearly thirty degrees over the last four hours, and the light rain that pelted the windshield on the way to the ramp had pieces of ice in it. Wind was a steady fifteen to twenty knots from the northwest, and the overcast skies completed the setting for what looked to be a perfect waterfowling afternoon.

The plan was to execute a small rig of a dozen or so black duck decoys complemented by half a dozen goose decoys. This size and style of rig emulated the population of birds that were using the leeward bank of Gray Cove. As I prepared to pull on the stubborn Yamaha 25, Finn anxiously sat on the middle seat, knowing that he'd be duck hunting in short order. He was more excited than I was.

With eighteen years of use under her keel, the old johnboat sported the scars of the years of abuse. Her bottom is a combination of Gluvit, 5200, JB Weld and assorted stainless bolts used to replace rivets that had been beaten out of her. The old motor, of the same age, sprang to life after a dozen or so pulls. Together, we made our way past the bar at the exit end of the Hammocks ramp. As the skiff found plane, Finn turned to face the breeze, ears and tongue flapping in the wind.

The northwest wind forced us to ride the trough for the mile or so before turning fairwind to navigate Rock Gut. With half of an afternoon ebb tide left to hunt, the passage across the skinny water of Rock Gut wasn't an issue. Most certainly, there wouldn't be enough water to make it through on the return trip in two hours' time. Knowing that the trip home would be a bit

Cold, crisp autumn evenings in November bring migratory geese to the mid-Atlantic. Winter won't be far behind.

longer, a bit wetter and a bit colder really wasn't of major concern. We were going hunting on a perfect weather day, there were a few ducks in the area and we were confident that we'd have a great afternoon.

Once the decoys were set, Finn took his place on the marsh, just to the bow of the boat. He sat patiently waiting for work; the summer of training had paid big dividends. Now a more patient, obedient and aggressive duck retrieval machine, he understood what his role in this game is. In one season, he'd turned into an asset rather than last year's liability. As the two of us sat silently staring at the decoys and the slate-gray sky in the distance, his patience wore thin after about forty-five minutes. He decided to go on walkabout, finding an old crab pot buoy on his adventure, which he quickly brought back to his station. Dropping it by his side, he resumed his post.

The feel of the afternoon was one of tremendous anticipation. Quickly, it became apparent that though the weather was damn near perfect, it wasn't going to be the steady action we'd hoped for. Patience would be the key on this day if we were to find success. Sitting, waiting and pondering are parts of hunting. On this day, my pondering took me back to my early days of hunting. My father was a stickler for getting set up early and staying to the last possible minute. He firmly believed that each morning we'd get that early "black duck shot" that the unprepared would not find. Hearing the raspy calls from their overnight haunts as the marsh begins to come to life just before first light only increases the anticipation of the possibility. He also believed that the same would occur just around sundown. His beliefs were based on personal experience. On this afternoon, Finn and I settled in, waiting for our opportunity.

In days past, weather such as this would provide steady shooting puddlers on the low water and divers when the tide rose. But those days are gone. Gone also are the numbers of ducks we once enjoyed and the numbers of local hunters who aided in keeping birds moving. Once, in a time long ago, the parking lot of Hammocks would have been full of trucks. Now only a handful of locals gun. Traveling hunters from all over occasionally try their hand on the public marsh. On this night, we were the only truck in the parking lot. That was fine with us.

A pied-billed grebe rose from under the surface of the rippled water. Water witches, as we call them locally, aren't a game species and spend equal amounts of time surfaced and submerged. Excitedly, the smallish bird skirted the outside of our decoys. Swimming in a quirky manner specific to that species, he quickly passed by our station under the watchful eye of Finn. He'd look at the swimming fowl, then he'd look at me. He did this repeatedly until the bird was well down the bank. Finn held tight.

The sun now touched the horizon. It was the golden hour. Time was short for this hunt, but memories could be made in an instant. This day was to be no different. Staring out past Bernard Island at the orange blob disappearing behind Tangier, I didn't see the six incoming teal. A whine by Finn alerted me to the opportunity as they approached the seventy-yard mark. It was a quick approach and certainly a wing shot. The six abruptly turned into the wind and began to gain altitude. But that's the demise of teal. The wind will cause them to hang in the air like apples on a tree. I picked out two drakes with the first two shots. There was no need for the third, as they'd successfully caught the wind and were now well out of range. As I returned my gun to its resting position, the little Lab was on the return trip with drake number one. Dropping it on the bank, he glanced at me for direction and was sent for drake number two. The sun was now half under the horizon.

As Finn neared the bank with the second, a lone black duck rose from the marsh 150 yards behind us. Flying low, slow and with a lethargic wing beat, he set his wings, banked right as he approached the decoys and was floating feet up shortly thereafter. Again, Finn was back in the water. Now standing, I watched as the last of the sun set in the western sky. The wind

Image by Joyce Northam.

had moderated, and it was a comfortable and beautiful sunset offset by the now clearing skies.

The old man has been gone for nearly a year, and yet each trip, something happens that reminds of the time we spent together in the blind. Memories of the mishaps, the good shots, the dogs, the hundreds of friends who shared our experiences, blind building, myriad warden visits—all play a part in each hunt.

He always was one I could count on. His "black duck shot" seems to be the same.

TIME

It seems that the older we get, the faster time slips past us. Now, at this stage in my life, by all means I should have more time to do the things that make me happy. Yet, like most, this is far from the case.

Those of you who know me know that I'm not much of a mechanical man. Electrical repairs, hydraulics, wiring, plumbing and construction projects that I take on usually end up a mess. I can build a good duck blind, but you wouldn't want me building your house. As I enter these projects frequently and with good intentions, I'm soon well over my head in need of help. When that occurs, I'm usually on the phone with Tom Wall. In short order, he's either walked me through the issue or is on his way over to fix my f*%k up. Each time he bails me out, we promise that we'll go fishing soon. Days turn into weeks, then months. The frequency of our fishing trips decreased with each passing year.

On a glorious Wednesday afternoon in October, I was homebound from Rehoboth Beach, Delaware, with an ETA of about 2:00 p.m. Things at work had slowed as the summer faded. Under the influence of a huge Bermuda high-pressure system, the bright blue skies were moved by only the slightest of breezes. It was a fine day to go rock fishing. Even the tide was going to be in my favor, finding high water slack just about two o'clock. I'd be looking at the better part of an ebb tide. Perfect.

Since Tom had just helped me out of an electrical jam I'd found myself in, he was fresh on my mind. I called, he answered and we hatched a plan. I'd meet him at the ramp at 2:15 p.m. The boat was rigged and ready; he would supply the ice.

Often, fishing isn't about the fish. It's about the other things experienced.

All I had to do was change clothes and step into the truck. Fishing had been good, and I was looking forward to the afternoon.

As per usual, Tom rolled into the parking lot a few minutes late on two wheels. The ticking of his work van testified to the fact that he'd been running her hard to get there. He grabbed his cooler and a couple rods and made his way to the boat, dragging his sweatshirt. He looked like he'd had quite a day. Stopping halfway to the boat to pick up the sweatshirt he'd dropped, he opened his first beer of the day. From all outward appearances, it was well deserved. As was this fishing trip.

After the pleasantries, we cut loose from the dock and brought the Mako up on plane. From the JL Audio speakers came the familiar sounds of Dave Matthews's rendition of "All Along the Watchtower." We sipped cold Buds and eased in to the better part of our day. No words were necessary. No need for idle chat. There wasn't anything really that needed to be said, as we were both content with the situation and the company. We were happy. We were going fishing. For the moment, all was good.

I eased the boat off plane and grabbed a rod adorned with a half-ounce white bucktail tipped with a chartreuse tail. Tom went with a red-headed three-eighths-ounce head with an electric chicken attached. I chuckled at his pick, made a few wisecracks and prepared to go to work.

As I was retying my lure, Tom laid a perfect cast just under the bank. His lure washed around the point into the mouth of the first rockfish of the day. I netted his fat twenty-five-inch fish and quickly deposited it into the fish box. After giving me a little grief about my earlier comments, he placed the lure in near the exact position, with the same results. Focused on trying to get in the game, I let him handle the net this time. His good-natured ribbing continued as we picked a half dozen healthy fish off the first point we stopped at. I held the boat in position until a couple of my casts went unrewarded and then allowed the prevailing winds and current to drift us parallel to the marsh. We drifted in silence, casting and catching the occasional fish for a hundred or so yards. With our limits satisfied, we went on to find new fish.

Rods were properly stowed, and we set off for the Ape's Hole area behind Crisfield. It was a bit of a run; new Buds were required. There was no music on this run, just conversation. That's one of the hidden attributes of a fishing trip. Friends can talk. The roots of issues are exposed. It's an opportunity for honest and open discussion. The discussions are often intimate. Chatter of friends, work, family and personal issues often take up the minutes between bites. Rides between fishing spots oft provide time for such as well. This was the case this day.

Speckled trout are among the prettiest fish in the Chesapeake.

I had a few small creeks that I'd marked for exploration. Today was the day to see what they held. Arriving at the first waypoint, I could already fish working around the downtide side of the southern point. Tom's first cast and each cast for the next five minutes yielded fish. My white offering was getting no attention. Chuckling, he tossed me a bag of Old School Electric Chickens as he was unbuttoning his fourth fish at this location. Two more casts yielding nothing, I turned my back to Tom, snipped off the bucktail and went with a pink head and the Electric Chicken offering. Slinging the first speckled trout of the day across the gunnel, Tom broke out in a big belly laugh.

"I told you!" he said. "You should have switched a while back!"

We continued to work up the bank in a northerly direction, finding fish just where they should be. Points and any outpouring of water from the marsh produced rockfish. Grass patches just off the bank harbored speckled trout. For a couple hours, we fell into what fishing is all about. The cares of the world were put on a shelf somewhere far from where we were. Our collective focus was on our shared experience. Fish were caught, fish were lost, a lot of shit was talked and we had fun.

Sailing back up the Pocomoke River, there was no moon to guide us. The clear, star-speckled sky and crisp October air made for a spectacular ride. Gliding across the slate-like surface at six knots, we were in no hurry to rejoin what awaited upon putting the boat on the trailer. Opening another beer, I commented that our ETA to Cedar Hall was ninety minutes.

"Perfect!" Tom exclaimed. I couldn't have agreed more.

THE HUNTER'S MOON

The splash of my third rig hadn't hit the water when the only rig that Bobby Graves had in play doubled over. As I began to retrieve the rig I'd just cast, I experienced the same. We'd been fishing about five minutes and were now tied to a double-header of trophy red drum. Both behaved well. There was no crossing of lines, no working around the anchor line and no excessive misbehavior at boat side. Both, however, made huge runs toward deeper water. Lines stretched more than one hundred yards off the stern of the boat.

Fifteen minutes after the first bite, Bobby's fish came to boat side. I placed my rod in the holder briefly, netted his fish and then resumed my fight. Quickly, he cleared the net and gently laid our second fish of the evening beside his. Both were quickly released, and the process of resetting our gear was engaged. It was an adventurous start to our trip, and we had a couple hours of sunlight left.

Each of the fish, like many others we'd caught over the summer, exceeded forty-five inches in length. Heavy tackle wasn't required. Medium action rods with 5000 class spinning reels were more than adequate to do the job. In the shallow, fish fight away from the boat instead of under it. It makes for quite a tussle.

With the tide on the rise on this grassy flat, our plan was to soak the last of the summer season's peelers and soft crabs in hopes to encounter reds, specks and whatever else happened by. It had been a long summer, but now at the end of it, we yearned for one more good trip. This night would be one to remember.

Left: With a large, downturned mouth, trophy redfish are designed to scoop up fresh bait off sandy shoals.

Below: Speckled trout boast two fangs and a mouthful of gripping teeth to catch prey. Their yellow mouth is a telltale sign that one's on the line.

We had the whole area to ourselves. No other boats were in sight. Under the full Hunter's Moon, our plans were to do just that. Two slot reds came across the gunnel. A fat twenty-four-inch rockfish followed. Holding a rod in my hand, I felt the telltale tap of a speckled trout nosing the bait. Speck bites are a bit different; they can be rather finicky. Tightening the line, I waited for what I hoped would happen next. Predictably, I felt the line tighten and the circle hook found its way into the corner of the speckled trout's jaw. Immediately coming to the surface, I could see the fish shaking its head furiously in an attempt to rid the hook from its jaw. Bobby was noticeably quiet. As I battled my fish to boat side, Bobby finally broke his silence.

Bobby and I have fished together quite a bit. He doesn't get overly excited over much and is as consistent as they come. What happened next caught me by surprise. As I was getting the first look at my four-pound speckled fish attached to the 7/0 circle hook, Bobby was busy fighting a fish of his own.

"Whatcha working on, Bobby?" I quipped.

"Big speck…real big speck. Holy shit! Get the net!"

Swinging my fish over the side of the boat, it fell off on the floor. I quickly dropped the rod and grabbed the small net and went to aid the still chatting Graves. We've caught a thousand fish together. I'd never seen him this excited.

The sun had just kissed the horizon, and its last few gleaming strands caught the huge yellow mouth of the speckled trout Bobby was battling. My first view of the fish was the huge gaping mouth adorned with a pair of quarter-inch fangs. The fish was now ten yards from the boat, thrashing wildly. Bobby was as excited as I'd ever seen him. At boat side, the fish dove, darting for the engine, but the net caught him just under the surface before he could make his escape.

Pulling him into the boat, I deposited the speck on Aqua Traction behind the leaning post of the Mako. Only then could I see the reason of Bobby's elevated sense of excitement. Lying there on the floor was the fish we'd been looking for over four years of fishing. Healthy, fat and stretching the tape right at thirty inches, it was one of the largest Chesapeake Bay speckled trout we'd seen. It seemed like the perfect time for a celebratory beverage.

In short order, we got back to business. What followed in the two hours that occurred after the sun set was nothing short of world-class fishing. Our battles with trophy reds were sporadically interrupted by smaller slot fish between eighteen and twenty-eight inches, which were kept for dinner. When the reds moved out, speckled trout moved in. Specks from three to six pounds were caught with regularity. There was no pressure. We didn't have

No fish is truly caught until it is secure in the net.

to worry about finding fish another day. This was the last of the fresh bait, and as the last piece of it was cut and cast out into the shallow water, we reminisced on the year we'd had.

Bobby began to make things secure for the trip home as rods were taken out of play due to lack of bait. With no bait left and just two rods in the water, there was a peaceful feeling in the cool October night air. The huge Hunter's Moon hung just off our stern, making visibility outstanding.

Knowing that the weather forecast for the next few days was for cold, rain and wind, we just sat there soaking up the moonlight. We'd caught plenty. Our cooler was full, and we'd released a dozen or so reds over forty-five inches. Sitting there sipping Bud Light Limes seemed like a fitting way to see the season out. Finishing our beer, we decided it was time to make that move toward home. We both hated to see this season end. As I picked up the rod to my right, I felt that familiar sensation. As Bobby began to crank his in, line began to scream from my reel.

"Whatcha workin' on, CL?" Graves asked.

"Bull red," I answered in a low, growling voice.

It became hard to fight the fish we were laughing so hard.

UNDER PRESSURE

No one hates a duck hunter more than another duck hunter. *Hate* might be too strong of a word, but the feeling sure borders just on the south side of it for many. I've often said that I'd lost more friends over fishing and hunting than any other aspect of my life. This year would certainly put this saying to the test.

Annually, we look forward to the October season to shoot a few wood ducks along the Pocomoke River. This year, with the launch of Tangier Sound Charters, it was difficult to scout the area properly, and when hunting season rolled around, it was clear that I'd only be able to squeeze out a couple hunts in the abbreviated season. Though hunting pressure was as high as I'd ever seen it, the number of wood ducks made it possible to pick up my three birds on each of the three hunts I was able to make. The true gem of this early season was to get the chance to work with my now three-year-old chocolate dog named Finley.

During his first year, he was just a young pup, making a couple retrieves. Year two was more of a training exercise, with him being somewhat unruly. This year was certainly different. He seemed to finally get it, morphing from a liability to an asset in the field. It was a welcomed transition.

The second split, aka Thanksgiving season, was just around the corner. Rockfishing had improved with the falling water temperatures, and my book of fishing trips was as full as I needed it. Blind maintenance was put on the back burner as fishing heated up. Sailing up Messongas Creek, I first noticed a new blind residing on a spot affectionately called "Our Blind." "Our Blind" made for some very memorable hunts, usually with Butch and

Late nights, early mornings and lots of preparation are the staple of a waterfowler's existence. It's much more involved than the actual hunt.

Anthony Thomas. It was a great spot to work with a dog. The well-concealed blind provided the setting for memories made over two decades.

On the last day of the 2011 season, we were picking at puddlers with such pace that we ignored the falling tide. Unable to move the boat from her hiding space, we had no choice but to wait for the tide to come back to us. We sat in darkness for hours after the sun fell from the sky until the January Canada goose full moon rose above the northeastern horizon. Black ducks came and went. A flock of fifteen geese was easily called to the six Herter's floating stools. In the piney hammock just to our left, a fox barked and screamed incessantly as he desperately searched for a mate. It was quite a relaxing evening. There was no danger. Immersed in the waking of a marsh at night is something that all should experience. Yet in exactly the same place that our well-hidden blind stood just the year before was a newly constructed box made from the brightest salt-treated wood, sheltered by a brick red Ondura roof panel. The elderly lady who had signed my permission slip had passed on two years earlier, the property was sold by the estate, and I was out.

Continuing up the creek, a second new construction stood unbushed on the crux of the creek, with a mud flat on the opposite side where I'd consistently found success over the years. Wood ducks enjoyed that area. I would enjoy it no more. A longtime local resident had retired from hunting resultant from age and declining health. Another new landowner, another new hunter up a creek that once saw only my skiff for three months a year.

The sun rising on another glorious day on the Chesapeake dawns full of promise and opportunity.

Another five turns to what was arguably the most productive spot on the creek stood what I'd heard about but didn't want to see. A fella in the construction business from Virginia Beach had paid dearly for the marshland just forty yards from where I'd hunted for nearly thirty years. He'll be hunting over a flat where I hunted with my father, sons and countless friends. His shot will fall where the ashes of two of my gun dogs were spread as tears trickled down our faces. This fella most likely has no idea of the value that this place has for me and my family and most likely couldn't care less.

The new app on my phone provided me his name and contact information. A more in-depth digital dive provided more information about the new landowner. Staring at the screen with this fella's info posted on it really didn't do me any good. There's nothing I can do about it. It's his land; he can do with it what he wants. It's a harsh reality of hunting. For the first time in thirty years, I didn't exit that creek at least once with a limit of greenwings. For decades, I had that little piece of heaven to myself. This year, as many as six rigs vied for the attention of the few ducks that traversed the creek.

I'm not sure why, but increasing numbers of hunters have descended on my little part of the world. Because I'm a curious person and want to know who's hunting around me, I make it a point to engage all newcomers. Though I've met some good folks with this approach, I've noticed a trend in many of the new hunters who have come to our sport recently.

Some are concerned about infringing on the rights of local hunters, but most are not. This year, I chatted with a group of Keystoners as they leisurely took their time unstrapping their boat, making certain the plug was in, and donned their hunting suits while parked *in* the ramp. Kindly, I asked if they'd mind moving their truck, as I'd already waited fifteen minutes and had a bit of a trip in front of me. Their response was, "We won't be long." As my blood pressure rose, my tone became more pointed. I had to alter my morning plans because of the delay.

That same afternoon, I was headed to feed my growing deer population and came upon a new Bankes 21 anchored ten yards from one of my box blinds. Upon approaching them, I inquired as to why they thought they could hunt at this location. Their response was that there's no law against it. I asked if they saw the twelve-foot box blind bushed with cedars in an otherwise brown marsh just thirty feet from where they had anchored their boat. They said that they figured no one was going to hunt it. The tone of the conversation was that they really didn't care/respect my blind or the work I'd put into it. It was obvious that they really didn't care about the money I'd spent to rent the land that the imposing structure is perched on. I

The eastern black duck is one of the tougher adversaries in the Delmarva marshes. Best chances occur early and late in the day.

requested that they pick up and move. They asked if they could hunt in front of my blind for the rest of their day. The nerve of these assholes. I've never won an argument with an idiot, and it didn't seem as though that trend was going to change on this day.

Engaging the motor into forward gear, I slowly circled around to an upwind position of their decoys. Placing my skiff in neutral, I produced a forty-pound white poly bag of corn, zipped off the top and drifted through their decoys. I could barely hear the sound the kernels made bouncing off their plastic scoter decoys due to their yelling and screaming. They even mentioned calling the game warden; I told them that I'd already taken care of that and their arrival was expected within the half hour. I don't think they'll be back there again.

Piles on social media seem to be the new gauge of success. That's nice, I guess. Bringing birds home, pulling the trigger and spending time with friends is crucial to the experience. Respect for the resource, respect for other hunters and respect for oneself are the criteria on which hunters earn respect. Some things that occur are beyond our control. New hunters should be aware that elder hunters are creative, have tremendous resources and are intensely protective of what they believe is theirs. Especially if put under pressure.

HOT SHOTS

The four geese fell from an altitude of five hundred feet to just off the whitecaps in under a minute. Braving the twenty-mile-per-hour northwest wind, they worked slowly toward our rig. Nearly 150 floating goose decoys had been strategically placed up this Dorchester County, Maryland creek just for this moment. Eight lifelong friends anxiously eyed the geese as the rhythm of their wings slowed and then ceased as their feet stretched out to reach the water in "the pocket" of our decoy spread.

"Guy, y'all take 'em," I said.

Immediately, he and his son stood up, took aim and squeezed their triggers.

Click…click was the only sound coming from their Remington 870s, followed by the sound of three generations of Porters—Don, Donnie and Cole—cleaning up the four geese as they tried to make an aerial escape.

Fifteen minutes or so before this scene unfolded, the shells had been removed from the chambers of the shotguns belonging to Guy and his son. A cruel trick, yes, but in the context of our group, practical jokes like this have long made for interesting trips.

Growing up in Sanford, Virginia, alongside the crew that now shared a pole blind was a wonderful experience. Some older, some younger, we all shared a similar upbringing. Things that we consistently did in those days would strike terror in the hearts of today's parents. Ritually, we'd rise early, pack a lunch, grab our guns and head out for a day in the marsh. Imagine, if you will, a pack of eleven-year-olds walking down the road with guns, shells and bags of decoys. Surely today we'd be, at a minimum, stopped for questioning. Back then, it was no big deal.

Water retrieves of large Canada geese are often a struggle for most dogs. Desire always wins.

Over the years, we've fished, hunted, traveled and shared experiences all over the country. When the opportunity arose for us to reunite for a goose hunt in Dorchester, we jumped on it. The good-natured ribbing that comes with events like this is not uncommon among friends.

A dozen geese followed the same path as the four earlier customers. The starboard side of the blind was the hot spot. We huddled among the cedars and pine trees overhanging the roof, watching intently as the birds fought the wind to reach our decoys. Coffee and pork chop sandwiches were set aside. Guns were at hand. As the geese drew closer, the click of safeties snapping off was audible above the shuffling to get into position. Flying into the wind there was no circling. It was a straight approach into the pocket of the decoys—a straight approach in to a gauntlet of fire that would allow only one survivor.

On this day, we were the guests of Steve Barnes and part of the Easton Church of God goose hunt. This annual event, pre-COVID, was a truly incredible event. Over eight hundred hunters and two hundred guides would annually take positions across Dorchester, Talbot, Queen Anne's and Kent Counties. Fields that were never hunted granted permission on this day. Proceeds of the event fueled scholarships for local students. Lunch was at noon, a veritable feast of all things that are good on Delmarva. In that gymnasium, six hundred hunters and guides would eat, socialize and bid on various items. The time was now 11:00 a.m. Polling the nine hunters of the blind, I learned that only Steve and I would attend lunch. With a few birds still out there to get to reach their bag limit, they would stay through the lunch hour in efforts to scratch them out.

Lunch was outstanding, and the auction went well. All the time I was away from the blind, it was all I could think about. Clouds began to form on the far side of the bay, and the wind picked up to twenty-five miles per hour. It promised to be an excellent afternoon in the blind. I couldn't wait to get back. Dipping out immediately following the conclusion of my responsibilities, Steve and I humped it back to the boat. On the quick five-minute boat ride back to the box, we could see that it was about to get good. Picking up the two geese they'd killed during our absence, we soon rejoined the hunt.

Taking my usual seat by the door, away from the starboard side of the blind, I could see a trio of honkers following a similar flight pattern. A couple hundred yards from the blind, they altered their course toward the port side of the blind. Picking up my old tiger wood Eastern Shoreman goose call, I could tell something was wrong as soon as it hit my mouth. A familiar burning sensation numbed my lips and tongue. I continued to work the geese. If their path didn't alter to the starboard of the blind, it was highly likely they'd finish well outside of range.

I continued to work the call. The burning sensation increased. My eyes began to water. The call began to make strange sounds as the numbing sensation caused a lack of "feel." I could hear snickering from across the blind. As I looked down at the cast of characters with water streaming from my eyes, it was all they could do not to break out in full-on belly laughter. I continued to work the geese until they finally found it more suitable to fall into the pocket like so many of their predecessors. With the call to "Take 'em!" I put the call back on the shelf.

Three shots rang out; three geese lay feet up in the decoys. I didn't shoot; I was too busy looking for milk, Diet Coke, brownies or something to put out this fire in my mouth. They'd apparently soaked the mouthpiece of my call in Tabasco for the duration of my time away. This fire needed to be quenched—immediately. Lo and behold, sitting just beside where my calls were laid sat a bag of Combos. With certainty, I knew that the cheese-filled pretzels would soothe the fire. As they hit my mouth, I knew again that something was amiss. Though the outward appearance mirrored Combos, the taste was more granular and devoid of flavor. The others in the blind,

The soft colors of the hunt are often overlooked. It's a game played for keeps.

who I've known all my life, laughed as I've never seen them laugh before. They'd laid a cruel trap, and I fell into it.

They knew that the Tabasco would burn my mouth. They also knew that I'd reach for something to put out that fire. They'd filled the Combos bag with dog treats. Snausages, to be exact.

This one I'll not soon forget. Justice will be exacting.

MARSH HENS

Standing on the dock eying the flood tide, I estimated that it would not be full for another hour or two at the most. The walkway of the dock was covered ankle deep in green sea water; the channel just north of the ramp was rippled with a hard northeast wind that pushed water into the small seaside creeks. The tips of the spartina were nearly covered by the rising tide. On a day when most were seeking shelter from the coming winter storm, we eagerly launched our flat-bottomed nineteen-foot Southern Skimmer in search of marsh hens.

If marsh hens didn't fly, I doubt you'd kill enough for an appetizer. They'd rather swim than fly, and their odd way of swimming is comical. With necks outstretched, they slap at the water with their chicken-like feet, creating a small swimming target. They'll dive quickly, rising into a mat of sea grass or other places to conceal themselves. They fly only as a last resort, somewhat labored, slow and direct for only as far as required to reach safety. Once airborne, they make for a challenging target for small-bore shotguns. A twelve-gauge can be used, but 20s and .410s add sport to the game. The limit is fifteen per man, and with the conditions right, it's a number easily reached. It was to be a glorious afternoon.

There's a small group of folks down in the lowlands of the Mid-Atlantic who are privy to this game. Marsh hens, sora rails, clapper rails, king rails, moor hens, marsh chickens or whatever name they are called provide the first real chance for folks annually to take to the marsh. It's not the type of hunt where one can plan weeks ahead. One has to go when the opportunity

Ready, willing and eager, this young Lab is all business in the field.

presents itself. When it's right, calls are made, and things develop quickly. When it's right, we best go.

On this afternoon with a nor'easter bearing down on us, we went. Donnie Porter had never been, though he'd heard me talking about it for years. This time, he took me up on the opportunity. As we eased down the Intracoastal Waterway, the waves slapped hard against the bow of the boat. With a little more throttle, we reached an acceptable pace where we weren't getting beat too bad. My chocolate Lab, Finley, took shelter behind the console. After a short ride to the south, I picked a small gut, killed the engine and began to push downwind toward exposed tufts of grass where our quarry should be hidden.

With water now covering the marsh, the only places for these things to hide are around old duck blinds or any other object where they can actually stand. Pushing up on a high bank, the first bird took flight. Rising slowly against the wind, the bird quickly turned downwind to escape our approach. Donnie, standing on the bow casting platform, was startled by the bird's rise, and two shots rang out, followed by a third when the bird was well out of range. A second jumped just as his final shot rang out. I backed him up successfully, and Finn was dispatched for the retrieval.

Twenty yards away was another clump of grass. Nothing. Fifteen yards more and a single rose from a floating mat of grass. Again, Donnie's two shots went unanswered. My twenty-gauge spoke once, and again Finn was on it.

Donnie was less than thrilled. "I'd have got him on the next one. You shot him out from under me! I see how it's gonna be. Every man for himself," he lamented.

Another high piece of land was just ahead. As we nosed the bow up to it, two found flight, and Donnie finally found the mark. I could see the relief on his face as his second hit the water. Two more opportunities in the first gut yielded three more birds. Things were off to a good start.

Firing up the Zuke, we eased back out of the creek, sipping sodas. That's the great thing about chasing these things. No need to be quiet. No decoys or blinds to bush; just two friends with one thousand acres of water-covered marsh and memories to be made. It's social, it can be fast paced and on a good hunt, it'll certainly get the barrels warm.

Just another hundred yards down the big water, we chose another small creek with higher grass bordering the sides. Eighty yards inside it was an old duck blind. Perched on a higher piece of marshland, it had promise. Killing the engine, we spied two trying to make a getaway by swimming.

Well-trained retrievers add to the enjoyment of the hunt. Their loyalty is unmatched.

Water-swatted marsh hens taste just like flying ones. The two were added to the bag. Arriving at the blind, our hopes were answered. Two took flight, then another pair, then three, another single. In no sense of order, six shots rang out, and the melee unfolded as we stuffed more shells in our guns.

We continued to pick away at them for another hour and a half before we reached our thirty birds. There were misses, there were great shots and there were some things that occurred that won't ever be mentioned again.

"Why haven't we done this before? I can't believe that this is right out our back door and this is the first time I've been. When we goin' again?" Donnie said with more excitement than I'd seen out of him in a long time. Checking the anticipated tide level for the following day, it appeared that it could be doable. With the storm bearing down on us, predicted to pummel us the following morning, we figured we'd give it a try.

But that's the thing about marsh henning. The spontaneity of it is part of the appeal. It's being able to go at the drop of a hat. It's about the guns, the dogs, the boats, the mud, the year's first experience in the marsh, the weather and the feeling of being alone on a piece of God's earth that few will get to see.

But you've got to answer the call.

HORSE ISLAND CREEK

After a bit of discussion, the plan was set to participate in the early morning draw at the Princess Anne Wildlife Management Area down on the southeastern corner of Back Bay. The plan was to convene at the 7-11 in Pungo, Virginia, at 4:30 a.m. on the opening day of the second season split. I didn't know there was a 7-11 in Pungo.

I shut off the alarm before it rang and set about handling the early morning chores. Easing out the door quietly so as not to disturb the rest of the household at such an early hour, I began the one-hundred-mile trip. A stop at the Fisher's Corner Red and White provided a second cup of coffee. The trip through Northampton County and across the Chesapeake Bay Bridge Tunnel was uneventful, with very little traffic in the wee hours of the morning. The Clash, Talking Heads, Springsteen and some Lou Reed aided in making the trip pass quickly. As the music played, all I could think about was teal, widgeon, pintails and assorted other puddlers that I'd hopefully encounter in less than three hours. The thought of hunting Back Bay for the first time made my pulse quicken.

I was sure that they were pulling my leg about a 7-11 in Pungo, but sure as heck, there on the west side of Princess Anne Road in the middle of nowhere was a beacon marking it as such. Wheeling in the parking lot, I was pleased to see my partners for the morning waiting outside the store with the familiar green, red and orange paper cups in their hands. Dan Arris, his son David "D.A." and Walter Potter chastised me for being ten minutes late. I didn't think that was too bad considering I'd covered 115 miles in just over two

Much like real estate, the key to angling success is location. A good anchor man is key.

hours. They thought otherwise. Quickly, I loaded my gear in their old Suburban, and we were on our way.

This whole endeavor was extremely new to me. Hunting in public marshes on the Eastern Shore was a free-for-all; first come, first served, with no holds. The concept of a civilized draw for hunting position was something I was anxious to experience. Arriving at the site of the draw, I was surprised to see fifteen or so rigs already there. Several more rolled in as we made our way into the facility. I was equally anxious to see the other hunters' rigs and how they'd set them up.

Inside the building, hunters huddled within their groups, discussing options and plans for the day. Planning prior to the draw, I thought, was of little consequence. We surveyed the map of the area, selecting five or so places we'd like to get to if we had an early draw. Otherwise, we'd just take the best available option.

Still trying to get a handle on the procedure of the day, I was instructed to drop my license into a rat-wired bingo ball cage type of device, from which they'd mix and ultimately draw licenses out. First drawn would get first pick, and so on. Thirty or so groups now were in the room as the appointed time arrived. After a couple of spins of the cage, a scruffy old employee of the Commonwealth they called Lionel pulled out the first name.

"C.L. Marshall…C.L. Marshall," he called. Startled, a bit confused and nervous, I didn't quite know what to do. They'd talked a lot about Cedar Island and something called the Trojan Marsh. Down a bit on our list were a couple locations on the Pocahontas marsh. I knew nothing about the area, where the birds liked to be or how to get to any of these blind stakes. For some odd reason, Horse Island Creek caught my eye. There were four or so available stakes in that area; I hung my hopes on a leeward cove on the western side of the creek. The other three in my party were somewhat indifferent about my sudden choice. Quickly, we exited the property, made our way to the ramp and launched the eighteen-foot Polar Kraft.

In the predawn, I could feel the wind freshening from the northwest. Although it was relatively light when we met at the 7-11, the chilly breeze now fluctuated between ten and fifteen miles per hour. The light cloud cover from the east would make for a late dawn. Weather wise, it was shaping up to be a good morning. There was some continuing debate as to the wisdom of my decision.

As the old Mercury fired up, we began to make our way through the unfamiliar darkness. Sitting back to the wind, I had no idea how long it would take to get to the selected location. From my vantage point, I could see spotlights everywhere. In my usual haunts back on the Shore, I'd rarely see another hunter. I'd seen more in the last half hour than I'd seen all last year. It was a strange environment. A slight right turn took us into what I assumed to be Horse Island Creek. Reducing to a slow troll, D.A. began to search the shoreline for the designated blind stake. Finding it after a brief search, we tucked the boat alongside it to get a feel for how we should lay the decoys. Quickly, we deployed a mixed rig of fifty or so widgeons, pintails, teal and black ducks. Satisfied with our work, we tucked up under the bank and began to make ready for legal shooting time, which would arrive in ten minutes. The blind was erected and cover added as needed, and in short order, we were ready to go. Pouring cups of coffee from the rusty Stanley, we watched as another hunter was busy trying to get set up. A couple hundred yards away, we felt as though as he'd be no threat to our morning.

As we were enthralled with this fella's endeavors, a dozen teal fell into the decoys, followed by three more. Finding us standing and chatting, they quickly fled the scene. With less than five minutes before legal, we made ready. Birds were on the move, and everything was falling into place.

Just after legal, our first opportunity came. Fifteen or so teal barreled from the open water by False Cape toward our spread. As they had no intention to land, we took our chances on the wing. They rolled in from left to right; positioned on the right, I didn't get in on the easy pickings, instead pulling a hen pintail from the hinterlands as they raced skyward. Just minutes later, the widgeon began to work the creek. Flocks from three to thirty consistently found our decoys welcoming. We shot well, not noticing how those set up nearest us were faring. By 9:00 a.m., we'd fetched a three-man limit of baldpates, a few teal and the one hen springtail. It was an excellent morning, which was rehashed over a hot breakfast at a nearby greasy spoon. Of course, I expounded on my guiding abilities, especially in an unfamiliar location.

After retrieving my car at the 7-11, we made our way back to David's home on Thaila Creek to properly clean the birds and handle the mess we made in the boat. With those chores satisfied, David and I headed up to the Shore for the Duck Unlimited banquet held at the Moose Lodge in Belle

Good gun dogs not only ensure proper game retrieval but also add a totally new dimension to the hunt.

Haven, Virginia. Arriving with the throng of locals eager to feast on oyster fritters and quench their thirst with copious amounts of Bud products, we were patiently waiting in line.

A bit tired from the events of the day, we stood silently waiting our turn while others in line chatted about their successes and failures on this opening day. A sandy-haired, red-faced middle-aged gent dominated the conversation in his group just ahead of us. Someone asked him where he had hunted in the morning, and off he went. Obviously from Virginia Beach, he went into great detail on how someone he didn't know rolled into the lottery, got first pick and then proceeded to hammer the ducks in Horse Island Creek. He talked about the shot on the pintail that fell from the heavens; he detailed how we wiped out a flock of five baldpates. He talked about how we were out of there by nine o'clock, certainly with a limit. He talked about how we sucked all the birds away from his rig. On and on, he detailed our morning hunt.

We didn't tell him. We just listened and laughed.

THE QUIET TIME

As I was standing on the bow of the Mako drifting southward on an ebb tide, the cobia cruised just twenty yards off the bow. I watched the fish move along; it seemed to have no reverence for the head current. Rod in hand, the quarry sighted, I entered the quiet time.

No JL Audio speakers piping out Whiskey Myers. No conversation. No one else on board. The calm, oil-like surface of the Chesapeake produced no slapping of waves against the fiberglass. High in the July sky, the sun provided excellent visibility—the perfect day for sight casting for cobia. With her dorsal fin just below and the tail occasionally cresting the surface, she lumbered along, aimlessly gliding along just below the surface. My focus was squarely on that moving target, long and brown. The high sun provided occasional glances of the whitish racing stripe painted down her side. She was beautiful.

The issues at work, missed phone calls, unreturned emails, engagement schedule for the upcoming weekend, list of honey-dos, overdue oil change or any of the multitude of pressing items that demanded attention—none crept into my mind. One cast, the fish and me.

It's in this zone that predators live. Now, alone in my thoughts, confident and well prepared, I find myself at the moment of truth. The other boats in the area faded from existence. Completely unaware of the others encroaching on my space, they really didn't matter. They weren't of any great concern. Time slowed, and surety of outcome depended on what actions occurred next. Much like a quarterback throwing a pass to a receiver

Outdoor adventures are made up of moments of action and long periods of anticipation.

cutting across the middle, the fish had to be led properly. Experience had taught me that the fish are moving quicker than one might think. Ample lead is required.

Checking the rigged eel in the bucket to my right to ensure that there were no tangles, there was no hesitation on what came next. With surety, the bait was sent airborne toward a likely spot where the fish would be. The eel hit the water and immediately began an attempted downward escape. Landing just four feet in front of the cruising cobia, the quarry quickly accelerated, and with a leisurely opening of its mouth and gills, the eel was quickly inhaled. Still undistracted from all surroundings, the fish peeled off line for a cool four count. The bail was instinctively flipped, and the line drew taut. Line began peeling off the reel, and pressure on the rod increased. A winter full of reel maintenance, tying hooks and leaders, boat preparation and dreams all came to fruition at this moment.

The fish fought on the surface, thrashing wildly, making a long down-current run that tested the newly greased drag system. This beast, likely well over fifty pounds, turned and hesitantly came toward the boat. Still on the bow, with rod bent, my first good look at the fish since taking the bait came as the cobia followed my lead to a point just fifteen yards from the boat. Seeing the boat, or possibly me, she sounded. A vertical fight ensued for the next fifteen minutes. Finally, at boat side, the exhausted fish surrendered. Head to the current, she lay with the hook lodged in the corner of her mouth. Stepping down off the bow platform where I had engaged the fight, I let her drift, with tight line, toward the stern of the boat.

She gazed at her captor, the forty-pound fluorocarbon leader in my left hand. My right hand slipped under her gill plate, and the hook was easily dislodged. As if she knew that she'd be rewarded for good behavior, she—oddly for the species—remained docile at boat side, staring up at me with her big brown eye. After a couple minutes, she regained her strength. As I

With a squeeze on the tail, most fish will let you know when they're ready to go.

grabbed her by the base of the tail, she informed me that our shared time was over. With a push, she swam off strongly and a bit more educated.

The whole event had taken no more than twenty minutes. During that time, detached from all surroundings, I'd become once again refreshed, renewed and ready to join reality. The predatory instinct had subsided, momentarily, but that time when my mind was quiet and without distraction or any outside influences was, and is, the epitome of time spent on the water.

I can't wait to get back there again.

OTHER PEOPLE'S FISH (OPF)

Social media has had a vast impact on our everyday lives. Somehow, normally productive people are sucked into a void for hours on end, hundreds of hours a month, thousands of hours a year, concerned with what other people are doing. On the fishing scene, nothing makes a fisherman more agitated than seeing another fisherman post a fish. Too much time is spent on the fantasy of catching other people's fish. It's something that will never be achieved.

Long before the whole social media craze, spot busting and searching metadata to find the latitude/longitude of where pictures were sent from fishing was somewhat more civil. On one sunny Sunday afternoon, we launched out of Quinby to fish the flood tide. Inside the inlet sits an oyster bar covered by twelve or so feet of water. With the incoming tide, the black drum annually make their way there to feast on whatever morsels they can find. Crabs, clams and other small crustaceans are all fair game. The fish aren't the largest of the species; usually forty pounds would take in the biggest. They're great table fare, absent of the "worms" that are encountered in the larger of the species.

On this day, Bill Hall and I launched a twenty-foot Chincoteague Island Sportfisherman and were quickly underway. Just outside the marina, we brought her up on plane just outside the dredged channel in Quinby Creek. It was four or so miles under the keel until we joined Sandy Island Channel and a bit deeper water. Continuing toward the inlet, with Hog Island in sight, we turned to the south for a half mile or so and brought her to idle as

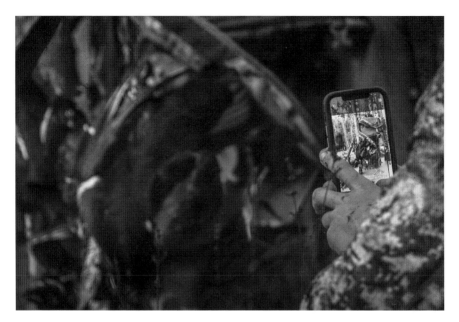

Kids these days. Downtime between flights is spent checking social media.

we watched the old Humminbird for the oyster rock we knew was nearby. As if on cue, the bottom contour rose from nineteen to fifteen feet, showing a jagged bottom structure configuration. With a couple of small circles to ascertain tide and drift, we soon pitched the Danforth over the bow and made her tight. Quickly, we went to work busting clams for chum and shucking the chowders to be rigged for bait.

Four other boats were angling for the same quarry on this afternoon, with at least that many in sight coming to try their luck. About a hundred yards to our west sat our old friend Tommy Shaw. He'd been there about an hour before we arrived, his time passed by nibbling on a bucket of Tammy and Johnny's fried chicken and listening to the Dover NASCAR race on the radio. To this point, his day had been relatively uneventful.

I've known Tommy Shaw all my life. Eight or so years my elder, he has always been a larger-than-life personality. Standing six and a half feet tall, 230 pounds of muscle in his prime, he was all heart. He was quite an accomplished fisherman, garnering several awards annually in the Eastern Shore Anglers Club. Today, however, he was having one of "those" days.

In short order, Bill and I had two rigs apiece in the water. As I shucked clams into a bowl for future use, I noticed Bill's lucky green rod display the telltale tap of a drum inhaling his bait. Seeing it just after I did, he picked up

Waves, whitecaps and wind are often willing partners in an afternoon trip.

With a tail that's made for power and speed, these fish can cover a lot of territory quickly.

the rod, allowed it to happen and set the hook. Above the din of Tommy's cursing and good-natured ribbing, we managed to tie off the first of the day in short order. Regaining focus on my rods after netting Bill's, I could see that my line had gone slack. A few cranks on the reel revealed what I'd thought to be true. A short fight ensued, and in a few minutes, our second was tied off on the same lead that held Bill's first fish.

Tommy continued to scathe us for our good fortune. We caught two more. He moved, cutting the distance between us in half. We caught two more. We beckoned him to come and tie up right beside us. He again cut the distance in half. Anchoring with his boat just twenty yards from our boat, I could smell the fried chicken and see the seeds in the watermelon he had cut lying on the transom. He could plainly see the drum tied off on our stern cleat, and that drove him mad. Though he'd moved twice, there were still no bites for his boat. With four now tied off, we didn't need any more fish. Working on a double-header, Bill held his at boat side until I could land mine. Both were released unharmed for Shaw to see. Another blessing ensued. It just wasn't his day.

After changing his bait, Bill cast far across the stern of Tommy's boat, snaring one of Tommy's lines on the retrieve. As Bill retrieved Tommy's line, I battled our eighth fish of the day. As Bill was untangling Tommy's line from his, I pulled my fish into the floor of the scow. Securing Tommy's hook firmly in the rubbery lip of the fish, I tossed it quietly over the side of the boat. As Tommy began to retrieve his line, we quickly became aware of the extra weight and fish on his line. A few choice words concerning his angling skill escaped his lips before he realized exactly what had occurred. He was certainly happy to have the fish since it just wasn't his day, but the way it occurred just didn't sit too well with him. Comments were exchanged concerning our charitable behavior and his lack of luck on this day. His replies weren't fit for print.

Over the years until his passing, we often reminded him of our good deed, and his response was consistent. But that's what makes the fishing community what it is. It's a unique situation providing the opportunity to create memories, sharing experiences good and bad and, in this case, giving Tommy the opportunity to catch somebody else's fish.

That don't happen often.

THE RED ONE

greeted the family as I'd done many times over the years. They were a happy bunch vacationing at a rental house in Saxis Island, Virginia. The first few days of their stay had been full of sea glass, Assateague ponies and general vacationing activities. Walking toward their vehicle as they scattered out, I introduced myself. The daughter went exploring the area around the boat ramp. It was apparent that this one was a free spirit.

Escorting them toward the boat, I began the probing questions to determine just what the afternoon would bring. The young man in the group, estimated at about thirteen or so, made the expectations crystal clear. "I've always wanted to catch a red drum. From what I've seen, now is the prime time to catch them in this area. Do you think we'll have a chance to catch one?" he asked. That made the afternoon's mission pretty evident.

"I'll do my best for you," was the best I could come up with as my mind raced to places where I could make this happen. I helped the four of them aboard the boat and stowed their gear in the dry storage area while running through the safety routine. Rule number one, as always, was repeated several times. Rule number one is, "Stay in the boat."

Half Moon Island was as good an option as I had on this Saturday afternoon. On a rising tide with a gentle southwest breeze, the ride around Sandbar and across the mouth of Messongas Creek was pleasing. Creedence Clearwater Revival resonated from the speakers as the son, daughter and mom sang along loudly. Dad positioned himself behind the console with me as we danced across the waters of the Pocomoke Sound. Upon arriving at

The moments before the strike require concentration and a bit of finesse. Missed opportunities are remembered longer than connections.

Half Moon, I could see a nice rip forming around the east end of the island. A sandy spit protruding from the island created the perfect environment for a wide variety of fin fish to inhabit.

I positioned the Mako just uptide of the swirling tide and began cutting bait. Four dozen peelers, properly chilled, would provide the enticement for the day. Quickly, bait was cut. Tossing the legs and shells overboard, I could see small spot and other bait fish feeding around the boat. Things looked promising.

My plan was to position the lines across the tidal rip just twenty-five yards to my stern. The first line was adorned with half a peeler, tossed to the inside of the rip and then handled to the lady. Before I could get the second line in the water, she was fighting a small rockfish. Quickly analyzing the situation, I downsized the bait and sent the second line downtide and long of the fish she was fighting. The rockfish were thick on the rip, and it turned out to be quite an effort to get all four rods out. Our rockfish barrage was occasionally broken by a speckled trout. Two hours into it, we'd iced four nice speckled trout and our limit in rockfish.

Over the last forty-five minutes, the adolescent daughter was constantly commenting on the "treasures" that had drifted onto the island. I constantly reminded her of rule number one but knew that it was only a matter of time before that rule would be shattered.

The decision was made to move away from the rip and on to the flat as the tide began to fall, and the mom's rod doubled and line departed the reel at an alarming rate. The telltale splash on the surface left no doubt as to the species. She battled the twenty-three-inch red drum to boat side, where it was netted, photographed and deposited into the cooler. Prior to the move, I had nosed the stem of the Mako up on the sandbar and beckoned the youngsters to explore the island. I figured that fifteen minutes couldn't hurt too much. I reminded them of rule number one and then instructed them to ignore it. It was amazing the amount of collectables that the two kids were able to procure in such a short amount of time. While the kids were out and about, the parents enjoyed a chilly adult beverage while overseeing the events.

But it was obvious that the red in the cooler was still on the mind of the young man. His mom's success only added to the pressure of providing the young man the red he'd hoped for. With two hours of sunlight now left, it was time to get back to business. The souvenirs were loaded and kids retrieved, and once again, the Mako was back on the prowl. We anchored forty yards off the western end of the island in a slight depression or slough that I'd hoped would serve as a highway for fish exiting the shoals. It didn't take long for that to prove correct.

As the sun began to fall in the western sky, we fought off a variety of rays. Cow-nosed rays, southern stingrays, clear-nosed skates, Atlantic stingrays and winged wonders of all kinds were caught with regularity for nearly an hour. Occasionally, we'd sneak in a speckled trout or rockfish, provided the winged bottom dwellers didn't discover the bait first. With about an hour of light left, they disappeared just as quickly as they came. For the first time of the trip, there was a lull in the action. Fifteen minutes passed with not a tug. Baits were checked and redeployed. It had reached the golden hour.

As the sun was about to kiss the water, all eyes were on what promised to be a sunset to remember. The father was the first to hook up. After he set the hook, he got about two cranks on the reel, and then things began to get serious. The son, whose sole purpose for this trip was to catch a red one, was rewarded with his opportunity. His hit like a freight train, nearly snatching the rod from his grip. The fish were uncooperative. We danced around the boat, dodging driftwood, old crab pot corks and assorted other sundries that I knew better than to put in the boat. Somehow, we kept the lines from crossing, and the father's first came to boat side. His fish was quickly netted and deposited on the floor of the boat, and the

Played to exhaustion, this shallow-water redfish is soon to be released.

The tale of the tape is told with each catch. The length, strength and tenacity of these fish elevate the experience.

attention then turned to the fish the son was continuing to battle.

It was obvious he was nervous. He asked, "Is it a red drum?" Knowing the answer, I made light of it, telling him to fight it like the last stingray he had brought to the boat. That seemed to settle him a little bit, but seeing his father's fish lying in the bottom of the boat put other ideas in his head.

I provided coaching as necessary, and he did a wonderful job of slowly working the red to the boat. As the fish broke water just ten yards from the boat, he gained a good look at it for the first time. Until he had visual confirmation, he had held out some doubt that it could have been a ray. Now that all doubt was removed, I could see a change in his technique. He seemed to calm with a bit of coaching, but as the fish lay exhausted just ten yards from the boat, he stopped cranking to look at it. It's a common mistake but one that often results in the loss of the fish. This one, however, stayed stuck on the hook as he gained two more cranks on the reel and I got the net around the fish. As I hoisted the forty-eight-inch beast over the washboard, the young man let out a well-deserved, "Oh yeah!" The excitement in his face sticks with me to this day.

Pictures were taken of the fish with the entire family. The son's was nearly double the weight of the one caught by his father. But the picture of the two of them holding their fish, sun setting over their shoulders, is one that makes fishing all worth it.

It's the stuff dreams are made of.

THE DAY AFTER

No alarm was needed.

There was no late evening prep.

There were no worries about cutting out of a social setting early to be certain to get some sleep.

There was no need to check the tide, wind, sunrise tables or temperature.

There was no need to call any kindred spirits inquiring about "what they've been seeing."

Yet, like the preceding twenty-two days, I woke from a peaceful sleep at precisely 4:32 a.m. to silence the alarm before it had the chance to do its job. My first thought was fear of being late.

The uninitiated may think that the end of the waterfowl season is a "hard" ending. The fact is that waterfowl season begins long before the first decoy is tossed into the water and extends far beyond the time when the skiff is backed into the yard for the final time of the year. As the season ends, the next begins immediately. Since it's a couple months before fishing starts, it is the perfect time to begin prep for the coming year. Decoys are removed from their totes and washed. Hollow plastic decoys that found their way into the line of fire are converted to foam-filled floaters. Those that have long outlived their useful life are reluctantly thrown into the "sea duck" pile. Lines are de-knotted and weights retied. Ragged lines are replaced. Each decoy is carefully keel wrapped for summer storage and placed in a dry, clean tote. Totes, divided into divers, blacks, puddlers and other, are placed on a shelf to rest until mid-October.

As the sun sets in the west, this young hunter admires the last bird of his limit. Tomorrow will be another day to do it all again.

Then there's the boat. At season's end, the boat is a wreck, metaphorically and physically. There are dozens and dozens of spent shot shells lodged under the flooring. Empty tins of Copenhagen, coffee cups, brush, Ding Dong wrappers, pieces of sandwich and other objects unable to be identified are emptied from the craft. And there is mud. There's lots and lots of mud. A trip to the carwash and a couple dollars' worth of quarters usually take care of the mud.

As much of my rig is old, the act of repainting is one that I greatly cherish. Some of my rig is over forty years old. Layers of paint chronicle the number of seasons they've seen action. The top few layers are mine. The layers beneath are the ones of consequence. Just under my rudimentary work lies paint laid down by my father. Under his, hidden by time, lies the work of my uncles. These are the layers that matter. Knowing that generations before me held these same birds caringly means something. Just thinking about those before me tying a rig in Drum Bay, down the Backside or under the bar at Fox Island brings satisfaction that can't be derived in boxes of Green Head Gear. Those new decoys that bob alongside these old Herter's lack soul. They lack character. They lack history.

Each year, we get sixty days. Some are in October, some in November and December and the balance in January. What we choose to do with them is left to us. The end of each season brings a touch of sadness yet prompts the memory of the year and years past. There's also a touch of joy in the hope that we get to do it all again.

AN OLD FRIEND

Today I met with an old friend. Like many relationships, I regret that it's been many years since we've spent any appreciable time together. The word *friend* seems homogenous enough but means many different things to many different people. It's also applied in varying levels dependent on the situation. Lifelong, childhood, BFFs, old, new, ex, with benefits, work, loud, funny, drunk, wild and late all describe friends that most have in their life.

The reunion of today was much more personal. Like most friends, we're content sitting for hours in complete silence, neither speaking for the duration of our shared experience. Other times, we've been involved in circumstances that few would believe. We've seen heavy weather that had us pinned down for hours and times of beauty that rival anything under the kingdom of heaven. She's been mistreated, left dirty for days on end. Yet after all these years, she remains faithful.

Relationships are generally based on mutual respect. Over the years, I'm certain that there have been many times when I haven't lived up to my part of the relationship. Only once has she failed to live up to hers. Only once when called on for support was she unable to answer the call. Each time we're together is a new adventure. Memories are rehashed, old exploits embellished and past time spent together cherished.

Today's reunion was long overdue. The exact reason that we drifted apart can't be pinned down to any single incident. Age, kids, school, college, marriage, jobs and the usual suspects could well be the reason for our separation. The duration of our time apart wasn't a planned endeavor; it just happened. Days turned to months, months turned to years, yet our bond remained. Time and distance can't erode such relationships.

This reunion wasn't planned; it just happened. Opening the gun safe this morning, I bypassed the Franchi, Super Black Eagle, 1187s and double barrels. Pulling the old Browning A-5 humpback from the back of the safe, I could feel her weight. I could see the scars on the forearm and stock from a fall when I was chasing a crippled goose with Bob Bloxom. The dent in the ventilated rib was a reminder of a failed attempt jumping a fence in Lenora, Kansas, chasing pheasants with David Arris. There's a scrape going through the "Magnum Twelve" cursive text on her port side where she caught a nail swinging on a flock of canvasbacks in an A.W. Williams skiff blind behind Bernard Island. The sighting bead was lost somewhere near Lake Philpott chasing fall Virginia turkeys with John Foley's father, who I've called "Puddin'" all my life. The forearm, cracked from use and the removal of all the friction rings, was worn smooth in places, and the hilt of the pistol grip on the stock was now somewhat rounded from time and use.

Image by Joyce Northam.

Some hunting tools are more special than others. Old Brownings hold a special place in the hearts of men.

Unfortunately, the new marks weren't from use and hold no memories. The wear marks from the safe were unsightly and made me somewhat ashamed of the neglect I'd afforded such a good friend.

It was good to spend a day with that old Browning again. I vowed that our next time together would be much sooner than later. Friends deserve better.

THE FIRST TIME

What time is it?
When will the geese fly?
Is that a duck?
Do you have any more of that chicken noodle soup?
How long can we hunt?
Can I blow your goose call?
How deep is the water?
Do you think we'll get one?
Dad, is that a bald eagle?
Man, those teal are fast!
Why didn't we get one? I'm sure I hit mine.
Can I feed your dog?

The barrage of questions consumed the first five minutes of our hunt. And it continued for the remainder of the afternoon. And it was just fine.

On a bright, breezy Wednesday afternoon, John Boston and his eight-year-old son, Colton, and I headed out on the Pocomoke River for an afternoon goose hunt. Ninety minutes may seem like a short to hunt to some, but with questions being fired at me at a rate of six per minute, it can get quite interesting. Hot chicken noodle soup slowed the salvo.

Standing there peering out at the expanse of dark water and adjacent cropland, I watched the interaction between father and son. My mind harkened back to an early morning half a century ago, when I was the same age as young Colton. I clearly remember the events of that day. Sleep was difficult. Wide awake, I placed the alarm by my pillow to make sure I didn't oversleep. Shutting it off at the first single sign of sound, I was quickly up and in the clothes that I'd laid out the night before for this very special day. Dressed and walking toward the kitchen, I was surprised to find the smell of bacon, coffee and biscuits wafting down the hall. My mother was certainly not going to let such a special occasion as this get started without a good breakfast. Dad and I ate quickly, said our goodbyes and hopped into the F-100 and made our way off in the darkness of a November morning.

I'm not quite sure what I looked like walking down the boat ramp to hold the bowline for my father as he pushed the fourteen-foot boat off the trailer, but I felt like a penguin walking. The overabundance of clothes combined with hip boots that were a few sizes too big made movement difficult. I certainly was not going to be cold.

As Dad parked the truck, I took my job seriously. Standing there in the early morning darkness, holding both the bow and stern lines, I waited for what seemed to be an eternity for Dad to return. In the darkness, I could make out imaginary images of all sorts of things that had my mind racing. As I was lost in my imagination, Dad arrived unnoticed and

Waterfowlers are a strange breed. The worse the weather, the stronger their desire to go afield to the rawest of places.

Image by Joyce Northam.

quickly hopped in the boat. The old Evinrude sputtered a few times and then finally caught spark, rumbling to life. After a brief warm up, I was summoned into the boat. It was the moment that I'd waited for all of my eight years. I was going on a real duck hunt with my father. This was really going to happen. The stern line was tossed to my father, who then helped me into the skiff. Taking my place on the middle bench, back to the wind, I prepared for the ride.

I remember the ride being all the things that I'd heard described by the men of the town. While sitting on the counter of Till Fisher's store, I had soaked in each detail as their escapades were relived. From my position, I could see the salty spray beading on the back of my father's slicker as he guided us through the darkness. The feel of the same salt on my face only added to the excitement of the day. Our little skiff, laden with a few dozen Herter's decoys and our gear, plowed through the waves, its engine straining at times to maintain forward motion. It was the most exciting ride of my life.

In the face of a strong northwest wind, Dad anchored the boat in front of the blind. I handed him decoys and watched him expertly toss them in what seemed like perfect placement. He told me that the spot the boat occupied was the sweet spot where the birds would want to be. I remember sitting in that old box blind with our small charcoal grill warming our hands, toasting ham and cheese sandwiches and warming our hot chocolate. I remember the excitement in his eyes as he informed me that there was a drake bufflehead in the decoys and to "get your gun." That same excitement was present as he told the story again and again to family and friends.

The sound of geese relatively nearby brought me back to 2021. Somewhat disoriented from my mental separation, I struggled to get my wits about me for a moment or so. Finding the geese that had risen from the Beverly Farm, from experience I could see that we'd have a great opportunity. A group of three broke off from the flock, lost altitude and began their descent toward our two dozen floating decoys. At a point one hundred yards from our decoys, they took full advantage of the boundary effect. With wings outstretched, barely moving, the trio was fully committed to our decoys. Johnny, Colton and I watched the whole event unfold. Colton was shuffled into his shooting position, Johnny at his side, as I called the shot. His single shot .410 sent his target to the water. A quick follow-up ensured that the deal was closed.

Watching the father and son share the moment reminded me of a similar situation half a century ago.

What I'd give to share a blind with my father again.

DOWN HOME

The calls started coming in about 8:00 a.m. Gunning was slow, and there'd been some talk about getting together for breakfast. The conversation was awfully similar in each instance.

"What you killin'?"

"Us either. Slow."

"We gonna have breakfast this morning?"

"Great. There's three of us. That OK?"

"Cool. See you at 10."

With a good supply of deer sausage, backstraps, pork chops, bacon and eggs, we'd be able to feed a small crew of hungry hunters. This particular day was an anomaly in the Saxis area. Everyone who hunted was out, and it appeared as though they were all about to descend on our hunting cabin for breakfast. Hunting being slow, we began the process of packing up to begin preparations. We agreed that hunting wasn't all about what happens in the field; it's about those who we make life bonds with.

Around the table sat fourteen of my closest friends, my parents and my two sons. We'd all been hunting. We'd shared a morning in the marshes and waters of Sanford and Saxis. It's the area where we all grew up. Though we'd all taken different paths in our lives, the common bond that we share would never be broken. We all shared a love of down home. On this rare occasion when we took the time to share each other's company, we again proved that our bond was alive and strong.

Another group who'd been deer hunting saw all the rigs parked in front of the shop and stopped in as well. We made room.

The journey is often as much fun as the adventure. Many things must work properly to make a good trip.

Several generations of Baileys, Porters, Marshalls, Thomases, Graves and a Krabill sat around a barn wood–style table. The elders of these families had experienced something that many would never. Coming of age in a time when friends were acquired through mutual respect, shared activities and common interests, our bond remains tight. Our relationships yielded bonds formed by our offspring. It's one of the things that make life down home special.

Over pork chops, sausage gravy and biscuits, pancakes, eggs and coffee, we rehashed old stories and made plans for new adventures. But this experience is not unique to us, nor is the place. Each outdoorsman has a place that he associates as his. Though ours is communal, to some it's individual. Down home may be a wood duck hole tucked back in the woods, a small tidal creek that yields teal and mallards, a hedgerow in a cornfield or a windswept point on the bay where canvasbacks and bluebills find refuge from the turmoil of the bay. It may be a place that once was or a place that we only visit now in our memory.

Down home may be more of a feeling than an actual location. The down-home feeling is often associated with simple, rural life. It beckons us to a time when life was unsophisticated. In this place we feel safe and accepted and are free to be who we really are. The various stressors of life can be put aside for

Sometimes there's little time for reflection between catches. Other trips provide plenty.

a precious few hours. Cares are put aside. Focus is plainly put on the location and the intrinsic benefits of just being there. Outdoorsmen who travel to such a place as this are lost to the world yet just may end up finding themselves. Game taken is far down the list of the criteria for a successful hunt.

The group assembled around the shop on this morning all shared these same values. At some time or another, we've shared each other's company. Some days we've returned with full game straps, others with only the satisfaction from time well spent. As the last of the dishes were cleaned, we again went on our separate paths. Electing for one more cup of coffee, I settled into an old office chair to reflect on the events of the morning. Dad went about whittling on a mallard head while deep in thought, chatting informally about the same. Finishing my cup, I began to make preparations to head home. There were ball games to attend, household chores to handle and social obligations to get to. That down-home feeling isn't something just sung about in country songs. It exists, it's real and it's similar in all who share the outdoor bond. The benefits derived from visits to these places can't be bought in a store or seen online. It's got to be lived.

Time and tide have taken their toll on the group of that day. We'll never be able to convene again. But that day, we lived well.

WIND

Wind is the friend of waterfowl hunters. It changes everything. For good cause, wind gives us hope. With it comes the promise and hope of waves of new migratory arrivals to the marshes and fields we frequent. These new arrivals provide a reason to brave the elements.

The northerly winds of mid-October bring the first migratory Canada geese. High flying in the typical V-formation, it's a sign that colder weather is on the way, the days will shorten and water temperatures will drop quickly. For Eastern Shoremen, the days of fall need to be much, much longer. Fish are feeding heavily, fattening up for the winter, and need to be caught. Whitetail archery is in full swing with the rut approaching, and stands need to be hung, trail cams erected and rifles sighted in. Duck blinds need to be bushed or repaired, decoys rigged and gunning skiffs readied. All of these activities are put on immediate hold if the proper combination of wind and tide provides access to marsh hens. Again, wind controls us.

Unseen yet powerful, it dictates our cold-weather activity. Hard northwest winds often lead to excessively low tides on the bay side. Each time this happens, it opens a portal to days long past. Wandering around an exposed expanse of bay bottom reveals a time capsule composed of items from the beginning of time until yesterday. Old bottles, decoy weights, Indian artifacts, ghost pots and fishing rods are shown the light of day only a few times per year. A morning spent "progging" in these conditions is time well spent.

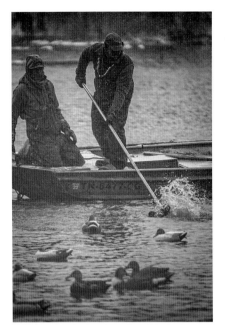

Decoys put out must be retrieved. It's amazing how quickly fifty decoys can be retrieved by experienced hunters.

The Witch of November is both a blessing and a curse. These low tides that proggers look forward to hamper access at many bay-side ports. Aided by these winds coming off the Great Lakes and points north, waterfowl take advantage of the free ride. Skies that were void of fowl seemingly fill overnight. Places that hold ducks traditionally are again blessed by the wind. Good hunters hunt ducks when they have ducks. Those who hesitate find that these ducks that blessed us for a few days are gone, quickly, without any sense of loyalty, on the next wind.

For those who hunt divers, strong wind is everything. Large flocks of redheads, canvasbacks and bluebills that form large, desirous rafts of fowl won't tolerate extreme situations for long periods of time. Small pieces of the raft will break off, and these birds will inherently look for shelter. This practice is one that savvy diver hunters are keen to, yet it's never that easy. Long runs down a leeward bank to such places require a sense of adventure that many don't possess. Setting and retrieving large numbers of decoys isn't for everybody. These conditions don't favor the ill prepared. Puddle duck hunters can't comprehend what it takes to be a diver hunter. The two require different skill sets. It's been said that folks are born to be diver hunters, whereas puddle ducking can be acquired. There's a big difference between the two. Diver hunting ain't for everybody.

Wind changes the way that waterfowl behave, which means it changes the way waterfowl hunters behave. It changes the many decisions that must be made in preparation for any hunt. It removes areas from consideration and gives preference to others. Wind's force goes far beyond its velocity. Small amounts of it are extremely beneficial, and too much is never a good thing—especially on the second day of a hard blow. These same birds that fell from the heavens before and during the passing of a front seemingly disappear on the second day of wind nearing gale force. We'd like to think they're still around, but most likely the same wind that brought them to us has taken them to another hunter down the line. The wind giveth, and the wind taketh away.

Every waterfowler craves wind. A passing cold front followed by a cold north wind provides the perfect situation for us to venture forth with gun and dog. Seeing the decoys come to life bobbing on their tethers in the shallows creates excitement. Thinking about the possibilities that wind can create keeps us moving toward the marshes and bays. It's these possibilities, it's these opportunities that we live for. Memories are out there to be made; wind is the invisible factor that makes many memories possible. From the boat ride to the challenging shots that it provides, it's all about the wind. After all, it's the wind that moves us.

THE BRIDGE AND THE SHARK

Growing up on the Eastern Shore of Virginia has its benefits. With the Chesapeake Bay at the back door and the labyrinth of seaside guts and creeks nearby, there was always something to do. Water-related opportunities abound. From picking up oysters to boat trips to Tangier to play ball, there was always something to get into.

As a Baysider, most of my exploration took place on the waters adjacent to our Sanford home. Beginning in a twelve-foot plank-bottomed muskrat skiff, my friends and I took many adventures down Jacks Creek. We knew every perch hole, muskrat lead and black duck haunt along its muddy banks. We knew where to catch peelers and how to transform a rank peeler into four or five rockfish. We fully understood the relationship between ourselves and the outdoors. We were the alpha predators. Young and full of piss and vinegar, we took to the outdoors like housewives go to Walmart. For us, it was serious business, proving our worth each trip with success measured by our success. We were serious about learning the how and why of our little slice of heaven. A little fun on the side didn't hurt either.

Skill sets were acquired at a young age that would serve us for a lifetime. As life transitioned, I had the opportunity to provide my two sons the same opportunity. It was pleasing to take my sons on that same creek to catch perch, rock and speckled trout. Such traditions are the fabric of who we are as Shoremen.

Trips to the seaside were always special. There was something seemingly magical about the saltier water, strong currents and rapidly changing

The moments before the strike require concentration and a bit of finesse. Missed opportunities are remembered longer than connections.

depth of the ocean-fed waters. A bit colder, the windswept barrier islands provided a playground like none other. Stretching as far as one could see, the strands of protective sand separating the ravenous ocean from the mainland were full of mystery. Many days we spent without seeing another human. Having access to such remote places, where we were just part of the environment, was priceless.

On a hot August day, my youngest son and I strolled along the beach break of Metompkin Island searching for washed-up treasure. Gill net flags, bright red poly balls, driftwood, a couple whale bones and a green plastic bushel basket were found and placed in the skiff. His first experience on an uninhabited barrier island was all I hoped it would be. We'd planned to spend the day just progging on the seaside. So far, it was going quite well.

The tide had risen quickly, approaching the last of the flood as we loaded the last of our treasure in the boat. With little current or interest in flounder fishing, we decided to opt for bigger game. Asking him what he wanted to catch, his answer was quick and decisive.

"I want to catch a shark," Parker answered with an air of certainty. I didn't see that one coming. We'd never been shark fishing before. We hadn't even talked about it. Must have been the effects of Shark Week that drove him to that decision. Assessing the tackle situation, I agreed, and we made our way northward back toward Chincoteague. It was a trip that I enjoyed greatly yet had made on only a few occasions. Passing the shallow Gagatha inlet to my right, sailing through Kegotank Bay, right at the entrance to the Ferry Docks, behind Wallops Island and under the bridge we moved along at a good pace. Our little eighteen-foot Chincoteague scow was built for just this purpose.

Just inside Chincoteague Inlet, we sent out three rigs equipped with two-ounce inline sinkers and 00 Clark spoons. As if on cue, a pair of small Taylor bluefish snapped up our shiny offerings. In less than a half hour, we'd put six small blues in the boat, perfect for catching whatever kind of predator we were looking for. I decided we'd make our play under Queen Sound Bridge. Why, I'm not sure.

Anchoring up tide, we sent our two-rod spread back toward the support structures of the bridge. Sitting back on the middle seat, I reached for a couple of Cokes from the cooler. Handing Parker his, I noticed the starboard rod tip produce the telltale tap of a shark chomping away on our offering. Parker picked up the rod, let him eat and then set the hook with all the skill and prowess of an angler far beyond his nine years. The fight was brief; the four-foot sandbar shark put forth an admirable fight, aided

Image by Joyce Northam.

by current. The exhausted shark soon lay at boat side, my son touching his sandpaper-like skin and admiring his rows of teeth. The hook was removed from his jaw, and the shark was quickly sent free. Our two other bluefish provided another two sharks.

Later that evening, our family loaded up the minivan and headed back to Chincoteague for a night at the Fireman's Carnival. Crossing the bridge, Parker issued the following: "I caught a shark under this bridge."

Fifteen years have passed since that day. Every time he crosses that bridge, he reminds us, and anyone within earshot, "I caught a shark under this bridge."

Another blessing of living on the Shore.

A CHANGE OF PLANS

S tepping out onto the pavement at Somer's Cove Marina in Crisfield, I wondered if I'd made a good decision. The southwest wind had increased to twenty-five miles per hour, and small rippled whitecaps danced across the water in the marina. By unsnapping the safety chain and hook from the bow eye of the Mako, the decision was made to give it a try.

Though the weather wasn't perfect, I was glad to be tagging along with my youngest son, Parker, and Charlie Coates on an early April scouting trip for big redfish in the shallows of the Pocomoke Sound. Though the water temperature was hovering around the fifty-five-degree mark, each of us had the time and interest in wasting an otherwise boring afternoon soaking bait in the shallows of the Tangier Sound. Besides, the Mako boasted a new 250 Suzuki that Sandpiper Marine had just hung on the stern, and we were all anxious to see how she was going to perform. It was an excuse to go—not that we needed one.

Idling out of the basin, it became obvious that it wasn't going to be a pleasurable trip across the Sound to the area off Smith Island that we'd planned to survey. As we poked the bow into the mouth of the Little Annemessex River, the southwest wind and the beginning of an ebbing tide created a tight chop that would make crossing the Sound a wet, bumpy ride. Once in the unprotected Bay, the long fetch would make for formidable seas once we found the deeper water of the channel just past the famed Puppy Hole. We could certainly make it, but it wouldn't be much fun. Fun was the object of this afternoon's trip. Alternate plans were quickly made, the Mako

Bent rods make anglers happy.

was brought to plane, trim tabs were adjusted and a course was set for Broad Creek. Our new plans were now set for fishing out the ebb tide behind the bar at Fox Island.

The new power performed flawlessly. Mental notes were taken on the fuel burn at a variety of throttle settings, and the lack of noise created by the old two stroke that had served us well for six years was obvious. "Stone" by Whiskey Myers blasted from the JL speakers as we found the calm waters of Broad Creek for the crossing to the Pocomoke Sound. Exiting Broad Creek, we kept her in the shallow waters, passing just off Watkins Point on our starboard. Ducking behind the old Doe's Hammock Island, we crossed the shallow bar and found the four-foot depth in Cedar Straits we were looking for. The bar would shelter us from the beating the southwest wind wished for us, making it somewhat comfortable to fish. The three of us were happy as we could be. Finding a fish would just be a bonus.

Setting the Danforth, the boat quickly snapped bow into the stiff breeze. A stern anchor was deployed and set, and the rope pulled taut, cradling us in a desirable position. The water was a bit stirred up, but the Garmin showed a water temperature of fifty-seven, and we believed it would warm another degree or two as the tide ebbed throughout the afternoon.

The three of us worked efficiently together preparing the sooks for bait, prepping the rigs and quickly getting fishing. It was just after 4:30 p.m., and all we had was time.

With the last of the six rods deployed, we surveyed the situation and found it acceptable, and I produced three icy Natural Lights from the cooler. Cracking our beers, the three of us huddled behind the console out of the wind, waiting for our bite. Right at the five o'clock whistle, we got our first opportunity. Up in the bow, Charlie pulled the rod from one of the port rod holders; it bent violently and then went slack. Upon retrieval, we surmised that the main line had wrapped around the brass eye of the flat three-ounce sinker and fish finder rig, causing the braid to break under the pressure of the fish. Zero for one. Not a good way to start. Quickly, we switched out the flat weights that we had set in favor of rounded casting sinkers in the same weight. Our thinking was that should the same thing happen again, the braid would slide off the sinker more readily as the fish made off with our offering.

We didn't have to wait long to test this theory. At 5:30 p.m., the rod tip to my immediate right began to bob and the slack in the line came taut. As the line came tight, I made a couple turns on the reel, sinking the barb

A bucktail presented on the "dinner plate" enticed this battle-scarred behemoth to bite.

of the 8/0 circle hook firmly into the corner of the mouth of our first red drum of the year. Line left the reel at a strong pace. Holding the rod high, I waited patiently for the first run to slow. As the fish exited the slough we were fishing inside, he turned parallel to the boat, allowing me to gain some of the lost line. Fishing for reds in shallow water provides the opportunity to utilize lighter tackle than in deep-water situations. An added benefit is seeing the fish thrashing wildly on the surface repeatedly, increasing in frequency as the fish is brought closer to the boat.

With us standing on the bow storage compartment, the fish fought to a stalemate at boat side. When we thought there was an opportunity to capture the fish in the net, he'd rip off twenty yards of line. This scenario repeated itself four times before Charlie secured the fish and brought it on the floor of the boat. Pictures were taken prior to the fish being tagged, revived and sent on its way, tired but no worse for wear.

A celebratory Natty Light was required. The first catch of the year is always special. It provides hope for the coming year and validation that our methods are still viable. Finding one near home in early April is an annual goal of ours, and for the last few years, we've been successful in making that happen.

As Charlie was walking toward the stern to deposit his empty into the trash bucket, the rod just behind him doubled over, line screaming from the reel.

"Charlie, catch that one!" I said calmly as he pulled the rod from its holder and engaged the fight. This fish fought entirely on the surface of the water, acting more like a white marlin than a red drum. White water flew as the fish ran off nearly one hundred yards of line, and then time and time again as it was worked closer to the boat, it would thrash wildly before again turning away. Our second was measured, tagged, revived and released unharmed. Things were going swimmingly, and we'd been fishing for just over an hour.

Good leader material is crucial in controlling the boat-side antics of citation reds.

Our rigs were again sent out in the little slough that sat just behind our boat. Subs were produced from the cooler, and we dined with no pressure. We'd already had a great night. It's easy to say it's not about the fish when fish have already been caught. Rehashing the events of the day thus far, we had no idea what was about to occur.

About halfway through his sub, the rod to Parker's right found his first fish of the evening. As he grabbed the rod and set the hook, the remainder of his sub was sacrificed. Watching it float off in the breeze and current, he split time between fighting his fish and cursing his lost sub. The heckling Charlie and I were giving him was interrupted as two rods on the bow went off almost simultaneously. Charlie grabbed one and I the other. From the outset, the fish behaved well, remaining somewhat apart as they fought for freedom. Things got a little more complicated as one more rod doubled. Charlie had worked his way down the port side of the boat and held a rod in both hands as line screamed off both.

"What do you want me to do?" he asked in an excited voice.

"Let one of them run. Put the one farthest out in the holder, and we'll get him when we can," was all I could come with as I focused on the fish I had on.

Parker's came to net first. I placed my rod in the holder briefly and netted his, passed him the net and then got back to business. Parker freed the net and the fish and then picked up the fourth hookup. Charlie handled netting of fish solo, as I held mine at boat side. The second and third of the evening were released, our attentions then turning to Parker's second fish. Seeing that he was going to be a few minutes, Charlie and I began to get the boat back in order. Tossing him another half sook, he rebaited and sent his offering to the opposite side of the boat from where Parker's fish was slowly making its way begrudgingly toward the boat.

No sooner had Charlie's bait settled on the bottom than he was hooked up again. To say that the last half hour had been chaotic would be an understatement. Netting Parker's fish and laying it on the floor, I then turned my attention to Charlie. He made quick work of his, which didn't provide the acrobatics of his prior catch. Pictures were taken, and the fish was released unharmed.

All our lines were now back in the boat after the ensuing melee. The sun had just begun its descent below the horizon. Most likely we could have stayed into the evening and caught a few more, but we'd accomplished what we had set out to do. Our goal was to spend an afternoon in search of spring red drum, and we'd found them.

The good numbers of redfish that we have today are reflective of those released over the past few years.

The rods were stowed for the trip in, but rather than pulling anchor and running in, we took a few minutes to relish what the afternoon had provided. The three of us sat on the gunnels of the boat, facing westward, sharing our good fortune and a celebratory libation. Watching the sun sink below the horizon from our vantage point was absolutely stunning on this afternoon. Our good fortune had some bearing on it; God's handiwork had much greater.

DEAD OR ALIVE

Standing by the fireplace, he had never felt more alive. The Eastern Shore had always been a special place to him, and on this day, he took full advantage of all it had to offer. Tomorrow, back at the daily grind, he'd return to normalcy. That bothered him.

The brisk late fall day had been spent in the hinterlands of the Eastern Shore in much the same way that his ancestors had done before him. November brings with it opportunity for Shoremen, and his lineage left no doubt of his standing. Arriving on a piney hammock of pines back in 1680, his family scraped out an existence from this inhospitable neck. Existence was dependent on success. Hard lessons were learned and passed down with care. The places where sustenance could be gathered, by any means necessary, were held sacred.

In such places he found solace. The places where waterfowl gathered, lonely places beaten down by the constant pressure of wind and tide, shaped by time and wildly remote, were where his most fond memories occurred. Small marsh ponds, old pole blinds washed away by the rolling whitecaps, spartina and cordgrass pinned down by harsh northwest winds and the headwaters of small creeks and guts were the places where he felt most alive. Special to him were locations that placed the rolling whitewater to his back and the calm of a leeward bank to his face. These remote places held the keys to his survival, providing fish in season, opportunity for waterfowl in the cold and mental escape from the grind on any visit. Trips to such places built him into the man he'd become.

First under the educational hand of his father and later with the company of his Chesapeake, trips to these places brought him as close to happiness as he'd ever been. When north winds blow and snow threatens, most "normal" people seek the refuge of their homes; he'd been taught to venture forth into the weather, knowing that success is often found when most head for the warmth of the hearth.

Waterfowlers seek these remote places. They yearn for them. Thoughts of desolate sandbars with divers ripping past, marshy creeks teeming with teal, ponds brimming with pintails and ice-encrusted parkas fill the idle spots of the day. Waterfowlers are not normal people. Aside from family time, the hours spent between hunts are times spent stuck in neutral. The Bay, marshes, rivers and fields breed life and the feeling of being alive. That feeling is addictive, fleeting and always in the back of the mind. These feelings are inexorably linked to such locales. It is these places where we strive to be.

These hallowed grounds that had shaped him into the father he was today provided the setting for much greater lessons. At times raw and unrelenting contrasted against calm, tranquil and soothing, memories were made during each. The successes certainly were relished, but the failures stuck. That's the harsh reality of life. Being able to live, as a

The sheer volume of decoys needed to successfully hunt large properties requires early morning labor.

hunter, transitions one from being simply a spectator to the wild into an active participant. A walk in the woods is simply that until a gun or bow is introduced. With weapon in hand, all senses are enhanced, sharpened and at the ready. Hunting in these places requires a different mindset than suburban hunting. It evokes a sense of survival, a primal urge to provide and a sense of adventure. It ain't for everybody.

The opportunity to spend time in places unshaped by man is a rarity in the twenty-first century. Places exist where one can be connected to the environment on various levels. Each of these places holds different memories. Each has a different experience tied to it. Some experiences are from human folly, others from the opportunities that nature provided. Some are solo, some shared in silence, others ingrained in our mind by muzzle flashes and the unmistakable smell of burnt gunpowder. Each experience is different, each individual to itself yet tied forever with places and people that it shared. The places will remain constant yet ever evolving. The visiting personnel will continue to change as time marches on.

Standing in front of that fireplace, three fingers of Maker's Mark in his cup, his thoughts bounced back and forth between what was and what was yet to be. The past 6 hours had been spent in the places familiar since his youth. The next 144 hours (six days) would be spent slipping in and out of the present. The duties at hand required most of his attention, his dreams fixed on what he had to do to return to that feeling of being this alive again.

THE PICTURE TUBE

I t started with a phone call on an early September morning. The question was simple enough.

"What do you think about going to Kansas? Turkeys and pheasants. What do you think?" David Arris asked as if he already knew the answer.

"Let's do it," was the answer he knew was coming.

With that, plans were set in motion—plane reservations made, licenses purchased, new boots acquired and a case of number six Prairie Storm shells put on order to be shipped to a Lenora, Kansas address. With each day that passed we were one day closer to a trip that we'd talked about for years. It was finally going to happen.

Coming from points all across the Northeast, we met at Jose Cuervo's Tequileria in the Kansas City International Airport. By their condition upon our arrival, it was apparent that Len Dillion and John Foley had arrived well ahead of David and myself. We hopped our "bathtub with wings" for a short flight into Hayes, Kansas, grabbed our rental car and were on our way. After a discussion with a member of the Kansas Highway Patrol concerning my excessive speed and their posted speed limit, our travel plans resumed.

Our sights were set on joining with farmer and friend Jared Mai in quest of pheasant, Merriam and Rio turkeys and good times with good friends. Lenora is a small town that, like many in the Midwest, is centered by a grain storage facility. With a population of about three hundred, a single facility served as the post office, general store, restaurant and bar. After checking into our rented house, we met Jared and a few of his friends at the bar to lay down plans for the morning turkey hunt.

Jared had ventured to the Shore the year prior for a duck hunt with the same crew. He'd never duck hunted before but fell into it naturally. He was enthralled by all aspects of it. The boat ride, the blinds, the decoys and the shooting were all new and exciting for him. It was a pleasure to introduce yet another hunter to the sport. We looked forward to reconnecting on his turf.

The location was a small operation by Kansas standards, only five thousand acres or so, and he had a pretty good idea where we'd find success. We'd be spending four days with him chasing birds. Just prior to leaving the bar, he mentioned something about a pigeon shoot on Sunday, the last day of our stay. He also said we'd have a hand in it.

Jared and I sat under a cottonwood tree well before first light the next morning. Watching and listening to the prairie come to life was certainly different than a marsh setting. Foxes, coyotes and other predators made their early morning calls and then went silent. As daylight neared, we could first hear and then begin to make out outlines of turkeys high in the treetops— first one, then another, then as light grew we found ourselves basically surrounded by no fewer than twenty roosted turkeys. Jared had certainly done his job in scouting.

He pointed out a big bearded bird just forty yards away sitting high in a cottonwood. There were no decoys. The first flydown occurred about twenty yards to our left, then another, then several more. The beast I'd been eyeing made his departure, from the limp, made a few pumps from his wings and began to glide downward toward a pile of hens that had made their way to a point twenty-five yards directly in front of us. I took him on the wing, and he tumbled into hens, setting in motion what could only be described as chaos. Turkeys were flying everywhere. A big tom took flight from the left and crossed in front of me at thirty yards. Reflex took over, and he was laid to rest a few yards from the first. As I took aim on the third, Jared put his hand on my receiver and said calmly, "That's enough for today."

Mid-morning found us walking up some ringnecks. Lunch and then a few more pheasants took up the remainder of the day. The scene repeated itself for the duration of our trip. On Saturday afternoon, Jared had told us that we were going to catch pigeons. None of us were real sure just what that entailed, but we piled into his truck with an ample supply of cold beer and Henry County's finest distilled products and made our way to catch pigeons. The truck was parked in front of an abandoned farmhouse. There wasn't another dwelling visible from where we sat. We sat on the tailgate and listened as Jared laid out the plans for our evening's activities. He said it was quite simple: just walk in the house, keep quiet, pick the pigeons off their roost posts and deposit them into the burlap sack. The windows were open in the house, and crack corn had been placed on the sills and in the house to entice the birds. Roost posts were placed in neat rows throughout the house where the pigeons would spend the nighttime hours. In the low light provided by the Goose Moon, we'd be able to quietly collect the hundred or so we needed for the next day's events.

The plan was working flawlessly, and we were going about our business with the precision of a well-oiled machine. That is, until Foley grabbed ahold of a sharp-shinned hawk that proceeded to beat the living crap out of him. His yelling and cussing and the general turmoil created by the hawk's assault caused an eruption of the remaining pigeons in the house resembling something out of *Batman*. Birds were everywhere, and from the sound of it, Foley was being beaten into submission by a bird with an eighteen-inch wingspan weighing about a pound and a half.

He quickly exited the house. Hearing him say he'd survived the assault, we continued to grab pigeons for ten or so more minutes. When we walked out, Foley was sitting on the front stoop, bleeding from various spots on his face, hands and arms. To his side was a half-empty jar of shine, and his eyes had that far-away stare. His condition was most likely a combination of shock, assault and the effects of the shine. Conversation didn't come too easily for him. He just sat there reliving the events of the night over and over in his head.

"John…John…are you OK?" David asked.

He sat there, taking another pull off the jar.

"He's fine," Hee Haw added in that slow Appalachian drawl of his. "His picture tube just went out."

The laughter that followed that comment was legendary.

DOGFISH

Tied to outriggers on either side of the eighteen-foot Gaskill Scow, the Coleman two-mantle propane burners hung just above the water's surface. Drawn by the soft glow, small baitfish, crabs and other assorted critters frolicked on the water's surface. Occasionally, a Taylor blue would slash through the throng, picking off an easy meal. As the biomass grew in size at the surface, so did the numbers of gray trout just eight feet down feeding on the oyster bar.

This wasn't a recreational fishing trip. Crabbing in the shallows near Saxis was drawing to an end, and David Bishop and I were looking to grab a paycheck from whatever source became available. Each fall for the past six or so years, those checks had come in the form of the fall run of gray trout. Using the last of our fresh-cut peeler crabs on top and bottom rigs, the trout were there for the taking.

This type of fishing is as basic as it gets: a medium action rod, twenty-pound mono, a top and bottom rig adorned with Eagle Claw 2/0 hooks held in place by a two-ounce sinker. With the changing of tides coming just at nightfall, the trout bite was as dependable as the rising sun. The soft-mouthed fish, ranging from two to four pounds, were eager to fatten up for the winter transition out of the Bay. Small pieces of peeler crab dangled just above the bottom provided the required incentive. The fish were willing, often coming across the gunnel two at a time. "Production hooks" we called it each time we dropped a pair into the saltwater icy slush that kept the fish in good shape until shipping the next morning.

Weakfish, aka gray trout, were once a staple game fish of the Chesapeake. Their recent comeback is welcomed.

As the sun set in the west on this particular slick cam night in early October, Bishop's Shakespeare rod bounced twice and then doubled over in his hand. Line screamed off the Penn 209 levelwind at an alarming pace. This was no trout. Fifteen minutes later, I slid the net under a fat fifty-pound black drum and laid him on the deck as the last of the sun slipped behind the distant Fox Island. Both in our late teens, we were living in true Eastern Shore style.

Time and the myriad changes that life throws at us haven't allowed us to share experiences such as that evening in decades. Yet friendships such as this exist mutually in our history and are rekindled with each meeting. That's what the Shore gives us. Whether it be night fishing for weakfish, gunning for geese out of a ditch in a bean stubble field or sipping bourbon in a finely appointed cabin, shared experience is provided by common interest in what the Bay provides. Relationships are built on this, and through it, lifetime bonds are cemented. Often as time passes we're drawn back to such memories at random times. The smallest, most insignificant things bring such experiences through our mind, and it seems it was "just the other day" when in fact it was forty years ago. Good experiences will do that to a soul.

Folks who live down on the many "necks" that jut out in the Chesapeake are a different breed. Fiercely independent, many are beginning to face changes that were never thought possible. It's this spirit that serves as a springboard for creativity and ingenuity.

Often, I think of the nights that Bishop and I spent anchored over an eight-foot hill on an oyster rock called Dogfish. Though the heyday of fishing for gray trout is behind us, annually I'll stop in there in late September/early

With the outcome of the battle decided, this big brute is prepared for his return to the Chesapeake. He's worn and a bit wiser for the experience.

October to spend a few hours experiencing that soft bite that was so familiar in my younger days. The fish are smaller, and the limit currently rests at a single fish. But each time the bait is picked up by the fish and brought toward the boat, against the tide, that old instinct takes over, and Mr. Trout is tricked once again. Each time one comes over the gunnel, it's hard not to smile remembering all the good times shared with many at this spot just two miles from the dock in Saxis.

At this same spot, on the same hill, I watched my father catch one of the biggest black drum I've ever seen. It remains the last spot where I fished with both my parents. The same oyster bar has yielded spot weighing one pound twelve ounces, croaker, speckled trout, red drum, perch and blues. More importantly, it provides memories. Memories of fishing there with both sets of grandparents and the parents of most of my friends come and go randomly. It's not as glamorous as some other well-known locations, but it's much more important to me. The fish are simply a trigger to relive the experiences that shape a life. I've anchored every boat I've ever owned on this hallowed ground. Places like this are special to Eastern Shoremen for what they provide the soul more than the cooler.

Using the last of the peelers we had, with three coolers full of fish and a couple of drum tied to the stern cleat, Bishop and I sat in silence on the center seat watching the lights of Saxis gleam just two miles northeast of our location. At nearly midnight, the full October moon hung overhead, bathing the Pocomoke Sound in a warm, welcoming yellow hue. Though young in years, we knew then that we were blessed to live in such a place. Words weren't needed. We were right where we were supposed to be.

THE BOOT

Well, it wasn't a snake in my boot, but it was close.

Some of the good things about the Chesapeake Bay lifestyle are the people we meet, the memories we create and the stories told about these escapades as the years pass.

Nine brave souls made the trip from all across the Commonwealth, both Carolinas and Maryland for a late December duck hunt. The center of operations was the shop in Sanford, Virginia, where my father spent his time carving working decoys and dispensing wisdom to those who wandered in. College buddies, fraternity brothers and a couple good friends who I'd met along the way had extended me several turkey hunting trips in the hills of Appalachia. It was good to have them on the flatland of the Shore for a duck hunt.

The weather was more fit for golf than duck hunting. A big Bermuda high hung above the Delmarva peninsula promising light, warm southwest winds, no cloud cover and abundant sunshine. Catch-and-release rockfishing could be a viable alternative if things got real bad. Scouting in the days prior to their arrival yielded no big ducks but an abundance of buffleheads. It looked to be a classic bufflehead beat-down for two consecutive days.

Things got underway on Thursday night with their arrival. We worked together to ready the two boats and then descended on the shop for oyster fritters, cold beers and the obligatory pulls off cold quarts of Henry County's finest Damson Plum shine. With a few hours of sleep under our belts, the boats were launched pre-dawn Friday morning, and the eight of us went to our two respective blinds.

It didn't take long for things to get underway. Situated just three hundred yards apart on the Saxis Wildlife Management Area, we could easily see each other's rigs. As the sun began to rise, the bufflehead bonanza began. Shooting from both locations was frequent, with multiple barrages required to subdue the cripples. With no wind to speak of, our shots could be heard for miles and miles. By 10:00 a.m., we'd claimed our respective limits. Communicating via handheld VHF radios, we picked up our rigs and made way to the dock looking for a hot lunch and short nap before the afternoon goose hunt.

Leaving the skiffs in the water, we made our way to the shop for hot bowls of clam chowder. Plans were made to leave precisely at 3:00 p.m. for the afternooner, and to a man, naps were taken in chairs, sofas, trucks and outdoor furniture.

Since we'd limited on ducks in the morning, the afternoon plan was to hold out for an evening roost shoot of geese returning to Bernard Island. The eight of us gunned over a single spread of thirty goose floaters from a makeshift blind constructed of crab pots, driftwood and other debris found on the island. Sitting on five-gallon buckets, we shucked oysters and waited for the afternoon flight. Shortly before sunset, things got underway. The first flock of six responded to the call, dropping to just off the water, and floated on outstretched wings into the pocket of the spread. There were no survivors. Retrieval was quick in the shallow water. A hard sand bottom provided solid footing.

Four more appeared low on the water. They remained quiet, as did my call. Movement in the blind spooked them a bit on approach, and rather than falling into the decoys, they turned with the slight southwest breeze, paralleling our spread. The decision was made to take them at thirty yards, and three fell with the first volley. The single was felled by a single blast from my Ithaca ten-gauge at fifty yards. With that, we picked up our rig and called it a pretty darn good day.

The next morning's hunt was a rerun of the previous morning's events. Buffleheads continued to stream in at regular intervals to both locations. The shooting, however, wasn't quite up to par. Those hunting around us must have thought we were shooting skeet rather than hunting waterfowl. At about 10:30 a.m., we finally got our last bird and headed in to end the trip.

Following a greasy lunch of hand-pattied cheeseburgers and fries, the visiting hunters packed their gear and headed for the hills. We'd had three successful hunts, went through numerous boxes of shells and reconnected on a level that only the Chesapeake can provide. It's always great to spend

A typical rack of a ten-point buck is the stuff that white-tail dreams are made of.

time with old friends, but I had another crew due in the next day and needed to prepare for them.

After readying the boat with the proper puddler rig for Monday morning's hunt, topping off the tank with fuel and oil and cleaning the guns, I placed my hip boots and gunning gear in front of the gas fireplace in the shop to be warm and dry.

Monday morning came, and I arrived at the shop early. The Mr. Coffee was engaged while hot water prepped the Stanley thermos. The high pressure had moved off the coast, providing a bit of northeast wind and increasing cloud cover. It promised to be a good day to hunt puddlers in Gray Cove.

Sliding in the warm bibs is always a welcome feeling. Gaiters bound the ankles as I slid my foot in my right boot, finding something soft, squishy and stinky in the foot. Running my hand in the boot, I retrieved a bufflehead carcass, now softened by two days in front of the gas stove. To say it was ripe is an understatement. My sock was wet from the ooze. As the smell rose from the boot, I hacked, spit, hurled and gagged for five full minutes. Both boots were tossed out the door as I wondered just who the hell had left me this surprise. Each of my guests from western Virginia received an early morning call on which I wasn't the most pleasant person. In the middle of call number three, my guests for the day appeared at the shop. I told them they'd have to wait until I finished the calls. I'm sure they thought I'd taken leave of my senses.

Thankfully, the tide was up. I wore knee boots that day.

ABOUT THE AUTHOR

C.L. Marshall is a lifelong Eastern Shoreman and longtime journalist. He's a former editor of *Shore Golf Magazine* and *The Fisherman Magazine*. His previous books include *Chesapeake Bay Duck Hunting Tales* as well as two cookbooks, *A Taste of Eastern Shore Living* and *A Taste of Delmarva Living*. To find out more about Marshall and his upcoming events, check out his website at www.chesapeakebaybooks.net.